⊲ W9-BHB-205

## SCRIBBLE
## SCRIBBLE
### *The New Bestseller by Nora Ephron*

The author of *Crazy Salad* now takes up (and puts down) The Media—from Dorothy Schiff and the *New York Post* to the great *New York* magazine/Felker/Murdoch convulsion . . . from Brendan Gill on *The New Yorker* and Theodore H. White on anything, to the incomparable Palm Beach Social Pictorial.

Here Is a Fresh Look
at Everything from
*People* Magazine to the
Assassination Reporters
to the New Porn,
Defined as "Anything People
Are Ashamed of
Getting A Kick Out Of."

Bantam Books by Nora Ephron

CRAZY SALAD
SCRIBBLE SCRIBBLE

# SCRIBBLE SCRIBBLE

*Notes on the Media*

## NORA EPHRON

BANTAM BOOKS
TORONTO · NEW YORK · LONDON

*This low-priced Bantam Book
has been completely reset in a type face
designed for easy reading, and was printed
from new plates. It contains the complete
text of the original hard-cover edition.*
NOT ONE WORD HAS BEEN OMITTED.

SCRIBBLE SCRIBBLE: NOTES ON THE MEDIA

*A Bantam Book / published by arrangement with
Alfred A. Knopf, Inc.*

### PRINTING HISTORY

*Knopf edition published April 1978
2nd printing .................... April 1978*

*All of these articles have been previously published
in* ESQUIRE *magazine, except Gentlemen's Agreement
which appeared in* MORE MAGAZINE.

*Bantam edition / March 1979*

*Cover photography by Harry Benson*

*All rights reserved.
Copyright © 1975, 1976, 1977, 1978 by Nora Ephron.
This book may not be reproduced in whole or in part, by
mimeograph or any other means, without permissiion.
For information address: Alfred A. Knopf, Inc.,
201 East 50th St., New York, N. Y. 10022*

ISBN 0–553–12275–4

*Published simultaneously in the United States and Canada*

Bantam Books are published by Bantam Books, Inc. Its trademark, consisting of the words "Bantam Books" and the por-
trayal of a bantam, is Registered in U.S. Patent and Trademark
Office and in other countries. Marca Registrada. Bantam
Books, Inc., 666 Fifth Avenue, New York, New York 10019.

PRINTED IN THE UNITED STATES OF AMERICA

*For Carl*

# Contents

# Acknowledgments

There is really no way for me to thank the many friends and colleagues who have helped me in the course of over two years of writing about the media. But there are a few friends who were consistently there: Barbara and Richard Cohen, Helen Dudar, Delia Ephron, Marty Nolan, Liz Smith, and, at *Esquire*, Geoffrey Norman, Don Erickson, Lee Eisenberg, Pat Thorpe, and Michaela Williams. To my agent Lynn Nesbit and my editor Bob Gottlieb, my gratitude and love.

# Dorothy Schiff and the *New York Post*

I feel bad about what I'm going to do here. What I'm going to do here is write something about Dorothy Schiff, and the reason I feel bad about it is that a few months ago, I managed to patch things up with her and now I'm going to blow it. She had been irritated with me for several years because I told the story about her and Otto Preminger's sauna on the radio, but we managed to get through a pleasant dinner recently, which made me happy—not because I care whether or not Dorothy Schiff is irritated with me but simply because I have a book coming out this summer, and if she were speaking to me, I might have a shot at some publicity in the *New York Post*. Ah, well. It's not easy being a media columnist. The publicity I had in mind, actually, was this little feature the *Post* runs on Saturdays called "At Home With," where semi-famous people tell their favorite recipes. Mine is beef borscht.

Dorothy Schiff is the publisher, editor and owner of the *New York Post*, America's largest-selling afternoon newspaper. I used to work there. The *Post* is a tabloid that has a smaller news hole than the *New York Daily News*—five front pages, various parts of which are often rented out to Chock full o' Nuts and Lüchow's. It also has a center magazine section containing mostly *Washington Post* columnists, a first-rate sports section and drama critic, and Rose Franzblau, Earl Wilson and Dear Abby. It takes about eleven minutes to read the *Post,* and there are more than half a million New Yorkers like me who spend twenty cents six days a week to kill eleven minutes reading it. It is probably safe to say that fewer and fewer young people read the *Post,* and that fewer and fewer young people understand why anyone does. It is a terrible newspaper.

The reason it is, of course, is Dorothy Schiff. A great deal has been written about Mrs. Schiff in various places over the past years, and some of it—I'm thinking here of Gail Sheehy's article in *New York* at the end of 1973—has captured perfectly her coquettish giddiness, her penchant for trivia and her affection for gossip. It is taken for granted in these articles that Dolly Schiff is a very powerful woman—she is in fact very powerful for a woman and not particularly powerful for a newspaper publisher. What is rarely discussed is her product. In Sheehy's article, I suppose this was partly because Mrs. Schiff had manuscript approval, and partly because the publisher of *New York,* like so many other men Mrs. Schiff toys with, thinks that someday he will buy the *New York Post* from her. But it is a major omission: There is no other big-city newspaper in America that so perfectly reflects the attitudes and weaknesses of its owner. Dorothy Schiff has a right to run her paper any way she likes. She owns it. But it seems never to have crossed her mind that she might have a public obligation to produce a good newspaper. Gail Sheehy quite cleverly compared her with Scheherazade, but it would be more apt, I think, to compare her with Marie Antoinette. As in let them read schlock.

In 1963, when I went to work there as a reporter, the *New York Post* was located in a building on West Street, near the Battery. The first day I went there, I thought I had gotten out of the elevator in the fire exit. The hallway leading to the city room was black. Absolutely black. The smell of urine came wafting out of the men's room in the middle of the long hallway between the elevator and the city room. The glass door to the city room was filmed with dust, and written on it, with a finger, was the word "Philthy." The door was cleaned four years later, but the word remained; it had managed to erode itself onto the glass. Then, through the door, was the city room. Rows of desks jammed up against one another, headset phones, manual typewriters, stacks of copy paper, cigarette butts all over the floor—all of it pretty routine for a city room, albeit a city room of the 1920s. The problem was the equipment. The staff of the *Post* was small, but it was too large for the city room and for the number of chairs and desks and telephones in it. If you arrived at the *Post* five minutes late, there were no chairs left. You would go hunt one up elsewhere on the floor, drag it to an empty space, and then set off to find a phone. You cannot be a newspaper reporter without a phone. The phones at the *Post* were the old-fashioned head-set type, with an earpiece-mouthpiece part that connected to a wire headpiece. Usually you could find the earpiece-mouthpiece part, but only occasionally was there a headpiece to go with it, which meant that you spent the day with your head cocked at a seventy-degree angle trying to balance this tiny phone against your shoulder as you typed. If you managed to assemble a complete telephone in the morning, it was necessary to lock it in your desk during lunch, or else it would end up on someone else's head for the afternoon. The trouble with that was that half the staff did not have desks, much less desk drawers to lock anything in.

None of this was supposed to matter. This was the newspaper business. You want air conditioning, go work at a newsmagazine. You want clean toilets, go work in advertising. Besides, there was still a real element of excitement to working at the *New York Post* in 1963 The paper had been a good paper once, when James Wechsler was the editor, and for a while it was possible to believe that it would be again. Mrs. Schiff had kicked Wechsler upstairs, had changed the focus of the paper from hard-hitting, investigative and left-wing to frothy, gossipy and women-oriented, but we all thought that would change eventually. At some point in the next few years, several New York papers would shut down. None of us really thought the *Post* would. "The most depressing thing about the *Post*," a reporter who once worked there used to say, "is that it will never shut down." When the other papers folded, the *Post* would have to get better. It would have to absorb the superior financial-page reporters from the other afternoon papers, the superior columnists from the *Herald Tribune*. It would have to run two more pages of news, enlarge its Washington bureau, beef up its foreign coverage, hire more staff, pay them better, stop skimping on expense accounts. Why I believed this I don't know, but I believed it for years. The managing editor, Al Davis, who once dumped four gallons of ice water on my head in an attempt to tell me how he felt about the fact that I was leaving the *Post* for a while to go live in Europe, was fired in 1965, and we all had several months of euphoria thinking his replacement would make a difference. Blair Clark, the former CBS newsman and thread millionaire, came in as Mrs. Schiff's assistant—he too thought he would be able to buy the *Post* from her—and we all thought he would make a difference. The *Trib* folded, and the *Journal*, and the *World Journal Tribune,* and we all thought that would make a difference. Nothing made a difference.

I first met Mrs. Schiff a few weeks after I started working at the *Post*. I was summoned to lunch in her office, a privilege very few other reporters were granted in those days, and the reason for it had mainly to do with the fact that my parents were friends of her daughter, and I suspect she felt safe with me, thought I was of her class or some such. "You're so lucky to be working," she said to me at that meeting. "When I was your age, I never did anything but go to lunch." Mrs. Schiff's custom during these lunch meetings—perhaps as a consequence of spending so much of her youth in expensive restaurants at midday—was to serve a sandwich from the fly-strewn luncheonette on the ground floor of the *Post* building. A roast beef sandwich. Everyone who had lunch with her got a roast beef sandwich. Lyndon Johnson, Bobby Kennedy and me, to name a

few. She thought it was very amusing of her, and I
suppose it was. She would sit on one of her couches,
looking wonderful-for-her-age—she is seventy-two now,
and she still looks wonderful-for-her-age—and talk to
whoever was on the other couch. There was, as far as
I could tell, almost no way to have an actual conversation with her. She dominated, tantalized, sprinkled in
little tidbits, skipped on to another topic. Once, I remember, she told me apropos of nothing that President Johnson had been up to see her the week before.

"Do you know what he told me?" she said.

"No," I said.

"He told me that Lady Bird fell down on the floor
in a dead faint the other day, with her eyes bulging
out of her head."

"Yes?" I said, thinking the story must go on to
make a point, to relate to whatever we'd just been talking about. But that was it.

In the course of that first meeting, I asked Mrs.
Schiff a question, and her answer to it probably sums
her up better than anything else she ever said to me.
The newspaper strike was still on—she had walked out
of the Publishers' Association a few weeks before and
had resumed publication—and I was immensely curi-
ous about what went on during labor negotiations. I
didn't know if the antagonists were rude or polite to
one another. I didn't know if they said things like "I'll
give you Mesopotamia if you'll give me Abyssinia." I
asked her what it had been like. She thought for a moment and then answered. "Twenty-eight men," she said.
"All on my side." She paused. "Well," she said, "I just
ran out of things to wear."

That was Mrs. Schiff on the 114-day newspaper
strike. She took everything personally, and at the most
skittishly feminine personal level. There was always
debate over what made her change her endorsement
from Averell Harriman to Nelson Rockefeller in the
1958 gubernatorial election, but the only explanation
I ever heard that made any sense was that a few days
before the election, she went to a Harriman dinner and

was left off the dais. She was obsessed with personal details, particularly with the medical histories of famous persons and the family lives of Jews who intermarried. I once spent two days on the telephone trying to check out a story she heard about Madame Nhu and a nervous breakdown ten years before, and I was constantly being ordered to call back people I had written profiles on in order to insert information about whether they were raising their children as Jews or Episcopalians or whatever.

Every little whim she had was catered to. Her yellow onionskin memos would come down from the fifteenth floor, and her editors, who operated under the delusion that their balls were in escrow, would dispatch reporters. In 1965, during the New York water shortage, she sent the one about Otto and the sauna. "Otto Preminger has added two floors to his house under my bedroom window," she wrote. "One, I understand, is for a movie projection room and the other, a sauna bath. Frequently, I hear water running for hours on end, from the direction of the Preminger house. It would be interesting to find out if a substantial amount of water is or is not required by such luxuries. Please investigate." The memo was given to me, and I spent the next day writing and then rewriting a memo to Mrs. Schiff explaining that saunas did not use running water. This did not satisfy her. So Joe Kahn, the *Post*'s only investigative reporter, was sent up to Lexington Avenue and Sixty-second Street to find the source of the sound of running water. He found nothing.

Ultimately, I discovered what union negotiations were like. I became a member of the grievance committee and the contract committee, and the head of the plant and safety committee. About the plant and safety committee—I was also the only member of it, and I think it is accurate to say that everyone at the *Post* thought I was crazy even to care. It wasn't precisely a matter of caring, though. I was physically revolted by the conditions at the newspaper, none of which had changed at all since I began there. The entrance to the lobby was still black, Philthy and the dust were still on the door, and there was a slowly accumulating layer of soot all over the city room. Then there were the bathrooms. They were cleaned only once a day and had overflowing wastebaskets and toilets. The men's room in the entrance hall still had no door, and there was something wrong with the urinals. In the summertime, it was especially unpleasant to walk past it.

I first began to bring up my complaints about plant conditions to management in the grievance committee. Mrs. Schiff was not present. I asked that the hallway be painted. I asked for a snap lock on the men's room door. I asked for more chairs and phones in the city room. I asked if it were possible to hire a few more maintenance people—there was one poor man whose job consisted of cleaning all the bathrooms and of sweeping out the city room each day. Nothing happened. About a year after I began to complain, I was summoned to lunch again by Mrs. Schiff because of a memorandum I had written about Betty Friedan. I asked her about the possibility of cleaning the city room and repainting the entrance, and she looked at me as if the idea had never occurred to her. (The next week, the hallway was in fact painted and the city room cleaned for the first time in four years.) Then I mentioned the bathrooms, which she referred to for the rest of the conversation as the commodes. She listened to me—as just about everyone did—as if I were addled, and then said that she didn't really see the point of keeping the commodes clean because her employees were the kind of people who were incapable of not dirtying them up. I tried to explain to her that if the plant were clean, her employees would not be careless about dirtying it. I suggested that she had exactly the same sort of people working for her as there were at the *Daily News,* and the bathrooms at the *Daily News* looked fine. I don't think she understood a word I said.

One more thing about that lunch. We were talking about Betty Friedan. I had written a memo about an article she had written for the magazine section of the Sunday *Herald Tribune;* I thought we could develop a series about women in New York from it. The memo had been sent up to Mrs. Schiff, who wanted to talk about it. It turned out that she was upset with Betty Friedan and seemed to think that *The Feminine Mystique* had caused her daughter, a Beverly Hills housewife, to leave her household and spend a lot of money becoming a California politician. Mrs. Schiff thought I wanted to write a put-down of Mrs. Friedan—which was fine with her. I explained that that wasn't what I had in mind at all; I agreed with Betty Friedan, I said. "For example," I said, reaching for something I hoped Mrs. Schiff would understand, "Betty Friedan writes that housewives with nothing else to do often put a great deal of nagging pressure on their husbands to earn more money so they can buy bigger cars and houses."

Mrs. Schiff thought it over. "Yes," she said. "I've often thought that was why the men around here ask for raises as much as they do."

Top pay for reporters at that time was around ten thousand dollars a year. Mrs. Schiff had no idea that it took more than that to raise a family. She had no idea how the people who worked for her lived. She did not know that one hundred dollars was not a generous Christmas bonus. She did not even have a kind of noblesse oblige. She just sat up there serving roast beef sandwiches and being silly.

Jack Newfield, another *New York Post* alumnus, wrote an article about the paper in 1969 for *Harper's,* and in it he quoted Blair Clark, who was then assistant publisher of the *Post* for a brief interlude. "Dolly's problem," said Clark, "is that her formative experience was the brutal competitive situation the *Post* used to be in. She doesn't know how to make it a class newspaper." In the lean years, she survived by cutting overhead, keeping the staff small, cutting down on out-of-town assignments, paying her employees as little as possible. And all this still goes on, not just because she still thinks she is in a competitive situation but also because she survived, and she did it her way. She did it by being stingy, and she did it by being frothy and giddy; she was vindicated and she sees no reason to do things differently.

The last time I saw her, she mentioned·that she had heard the things I said about her on the radio. "Nora," she said to me, "you know perfectly well you learned a great deal at the *Post*." But of course I did. I even loved working there. But that's not the point. The point is the product.

### *Nora Ephron's Beef Borscht*

Put 3 pounds of beef chuck cut for stew and a couple of soupbones into a large pot. Add 2 onions, quartered, and 6 cups beef broth and bring to a boil, simmering 15 minutes and skimming off the scum. Add 2 cups tomato juice, the juice from a 1-pound can of julienne beets, salt, pepper, the juice of 1 lemon, 1 tablespoon cider vinegar, 2 tablespoons brown sugar, and bring to a boil. Then simmer slowly for 2½ hours until the beef is tender. Add the beets left over from the beet juice, and another can of beets and juice. Serve with huge amounts of sour cream, chopped dill, boiled potatoes and pumpernickel bread. Serves six.

*April, 1975*

# *People* Magazine

The people over at *People* get all riled up if anyone suggests that *People* is a direct descendant of anything at all. You do not even have to suggest that it is; the first words anyone over there says, *insists,* really, is that *People* is *not* a spin-off of the *Time* "People" section (which they are right about), and that it is *not* a reincarnation of *Life* (which they are, at least in part, wrong about). *People,* they tell you, is an original thing. Distinctive. Different. Unto itself. They make it sound a lot like a cigarette.

*People* was introduced by Time Inc. a year ago, and at last reports it was selling 1,250,000 copies a week, all of them on newsstands. It is the first national weekly that has been launched since *Sports Illustrated* in 1954, and it will probably lose some three million dollars in its first year, a sum that fazes no one at Time Inc., since it is right on target. *Sports Illustrated* lost twenty-six million in the ten years before it turned the corner, and *People* is expected to lose considerably less and turn the corner considerably quicker. There is probably something to be said for all this—something about how healthy it is for the magazine business that a thing like this is happening, a new magazine with good prospects and no nudity that interests over a million readers a week—but I'm not sure that I am the person who is going to say it. *People* makes me grouchy, and I have been trying for months to figure out why. I do read it. I read it in the exact way its editors intend me to—straight through without stopping. I buy it in airline terminals, and I find that if I start reading it at the moment I am seated on the Eastern shuttle, it lasts until shortly before takeoff. This means that its time span is approximately five minutes longer than the *New York Post* on a day with a good Rose Franzblau column, and five minutes less than *Rona Barrett's Gossip,* which in any case is not available at the Eastern shuttle terminal in La Guardia Airport.

My problem with the magazine is not that I think it is harmful or dangerous or anything of the sort. It's almost not worth getting upset about. It's a potato chip. A snack. Empty calories. Which would be fine, really —I like potato chips. But they make you feel lousy afterward too.

*People* is a product of something called the Magazine Development Group at Time Inc., which has been laboring for several years to come up with new magazines and has brought forth *Money* and two rejected dummy magazines, one on photography, the other on show business. The approach this group takes is a unique one in today's magazine business: Most magazines tend to be about a sensibility rather than a subject, and tend to be dominated not by a group but by one editor and his or her concept of what that sensibility is. In any event, the idea for *People*—which was a simple, five-word idea: let's-call-a-magazine-*People*— started kicking around the halls of Time Inc. a couple of years ago. Some people, mainly Clare Boothe Luce, think it originated with Clare Boothe Luce; others seem to lean toward a great-idea-whose-time-has-come theory, not unlike the Big Bang, and they say that if anyone thought of it at all (which they are not sure of), it was Andrew Heiskell, Time Inc.'s chairman of the board. But the credit probably belongs, in some transcendental way, to Kierkegaard, who in 1846 said that in time, all anyone would be interested in was gossip.

From the beginning, *People* was conceived as an inexpensive magazine—cheap to produce and cheap to buy. There would be a small staff. Low overhead. Stringers. No color photographs except for the cover. It was intended to be sold only on newsstands—thus eliminating the escalating cost of mailing the magazine to subscribers and mailing the subscribers reminders to renew their subscriptions. It was clear that the magazine would have to have a very strong appeal for women; an increasing proportion of newsstands in this country are in supermarkets. Its direct competitor for rack space at the check-out counter was the *National Enquirer*. A pilot issue of the magazine, with Richard Burton and Elizabeth Taylor on the cover, was produced in August, 1973, and test-marketed in seven cities, and it is the pride of the Time Inc. marketing department that this was done in the exact way Procter & Gamble introduces a new toilet paper. When Malcolm B. Ochs, marketing director of the Magazine Development Group at Time Inc., speaks about *People,* he talks about selling "packaged goods" and "one million units a week" and "perishable products." This sort of talk is not really surprising—I have spent enough time around magazine salesmen to know they would all be more comfortable selling tomatoes—but it is nonetheless a depressing development.

The second major decision that was arrived at early on was to keep the stories short. "We always want to leave people wishing for more," says Richard B. Stolley, *People*'s managing editor. This is a perfectly valid editorial slogan, but what Stolley does not seem willing to admit is the reason for it, which is that *People* is essentially a magazine for people who don't like to read. The people at *People* seem to believe that people who read *People* have the shortest attention spans in the world. *Time* and *Life* started out this way too, but both of them managed to rise above their original intentions.

The incarnation of *Life* that *People* most resembles is not the early era, where photographs dominated, nor even the middle-to-late period, when the photography and journalism struck a nice balance, but the last desperate days, when Ralph Graves was trying to save the magazine from what turned out to be its inevitable death. This is not the time to go into Graves's most serious and abhorrent editorial decision, which was to eliminate the *Life* Great Dinners series; what I want to talk about instead is his decision to shorten the articles. There are people over at the Time-Life Building, defenders of Graves, who insist he did this for reasons of economy—there was no room for long pieces in a magazine that was losing advertising and therefore editorial pages—but Graves himself refuses to be so defended. He claims he shortened the articles because he believes in short articles. And the result, in the case of *Life,* was a magazine that did nothing terribly well.

People has this exact quality—and I'm not exactly sure why. I have nothing against short articles, and no desire to read more than 1500 words or so on most of the personalities *People* profiles. In fact, in the case of a number of those personalities—and here the name of Telly Savalas springs instantly to mind—a caption would suffice. I have no quarrel with the writing in the magazine, which is slick and perfectly competent. I wouldn't mind if *People* were just a picture magazine, if I could at least see the pictures; there is an indefinable something in its art direction that makes the magazine look remarkably like the centerfold of the *Daily News.* And I wouldn't even mind if it were a fan magazine for grownups—if it delivered the goods. But the real problem is that when I finish reading *People,* I always feel that I have just spent four days in Los Angeles. *Women's Wear Daily* at least makes me feel dirty; *People* makes me feel that I haven't read or learned or seen anything at all. I don't think this is what Richard Stolley means when he says he wants to leave his readers wanting more: I tend to be left feeling that I haven't gotten anything in the first place. And even this feeling is hard to pinpoint; I am looking at a recent issue of *People,* with Hugh Hefner on the cover, and I can't really say I didn't learn anything in it: On page 6 it says that Hefner told his unauthorized biographer that he once had a homosexual experience. I didn't actually know that before reading *People,* but somehow it doesn't surprise me.

Worst of all—yes, there is a worst of all—I end up feeling glutted with celebrity. I stopped reading movie magazines in the beauty parlor a couple of years ago because I could not accommodate any more information about something called the Lennon Sisters. I had got to the point where I thought I knew what celebrity was—celebrity was anyone I would stand up in a restaurant and stare at. I had whittled the list down to Marlon Brando, Mary Tyler Moore and Angelo "Gyp" DeCarlo, and I was fairly happy. Now I am confronted with *People,* and the plain fact is that a celebrity is anyone *People* writes about; I know the magazine is filling some nameless, bottomless pit of need for gossip and names, but I haven't got room in my life for so many lights.

*People*'s only serious financial difficulty at this point is in attracting advertisers, and one of the reasons the people at *People* think they are having trouble doing so is that their advertisers don't know who the *People* reader is. Time Inc. has issued a demographic survey which shows that *People*'s readers are upscale, whatever that means, and that 48 percent of them have been to college. I never believe these surveys— *Playboy* and *Penthouse* have them, and theirs show that their readers are mainly interested in the fine fiction; in any case, I suspect that *People*'s real problem with advertisers is not that they don't know who's reading the magazine, but that they know exactly who's reading it. In one recent issue there are three liquor ads —for Seagram's Seven Crown, Jim Beam and a bottled cocktail called the Brass Monkey, all of them brands bought predominantly by the blue-collar middle class. It's logical that these brands would buy space in *People*—liquor companies can't advertise on television. But any product that could would probably do better to reach nonreaders through the mass-market women's magazines, which at least sit around all month, or on television itself.

"The human element really is being neglected in national reporting," says Richard Stolley. "The better newspapers and magazines deal more and more with events and issues and debates. The human beings caught up in them simply get squelched. If we can bring a human being out of a massive event, then we've done what I want to do." I don't really object to this philosophy—I'm not sure that I agree with it, but I don't object to it. But it seems a shame that so much of the reporting of the so-called human element in *People* is aimed at the lowest common denominator of the also-so-called human element, that all this coverage of humanity has to be at the expense of the issues and events and ideas involved. It seems even sadder that there seems to be no stopping it. *People* is the future, and it works, and that makes me grouchiest of all.

*March, 1975*

# The *Palm Beach Social Pictorial*

I am sitting here thinking a mundane thought, which is that one picture is worth a thousand words. The reason I am sitting here thinking this is that I am looking at one picture, a picture of someone named Mignon Roscher Gardner on the cover of the *Palm Beach Social Pictorial,* and I cannot think how to describe it to you, how to convey the feeling I get from looking at this picture and in fact every other full-color picture that has ever appeared on the cover of this publication.

The *Palm Beach Social Pictorial* appears weekly throughout the winter season in Palm Beach and I get it in the mail because a friend of mine named Liz Smith writes a column in it and has it sent to me. There are several dozen of us on Liz Smith's list, and I think it is safe to say that we all believe that the *Palm Beach Social Pictorial* is the most wonderful publication in America. Beyond that, each of us is very nearly obsessed with the people in it. My particular obsession is Mignon Roscher Gardner, but from time to time I am unfaithful to her, and I get involved instead with the life of Anky Von Boythan Revson Johnson, who seems to live in a turban, or Mrs. Woolworth Donahue, who apparently never goes anywhere without her two Great Danes nuzzling her lap. One friend of mine is so taken with Helene (Mrs. Roy) Tuchbreiter and her goo-goo-googly eyes that he once made an entire collage of pictures of her face.

Mignon Roscher Gardner, who happens to be a painter of indeterminate age and platinum-blond hair, has appeared on the cover of the *Pictorial* twice in the last year, both times decked in ostrich feathers. Anyone who appears on the cover of the *Pictorial* pays a nominal sum to do so; Mrs. Gardner's appearances usually coincide with an opening of her paintings in Palm Beach, although the last one merely coincided with the completion of her portrait of Dr. Josephine E. Raeppel, librarian emeritus of Albright College in Reading, Pennsylvania. Most of the painters whose work appears on the cover of the *Pictorial* are referred to as "famed, international" painters, but Mrs. Gardner is a local, and the furthest the *Pictorial* will go in the famed-international department is to call her prominent. "Prominent artist-aviatrix," for example—that's what they called her last February, when she appeared on the cover in her hair and turquoise ostrich feathers along with a painting from a new series she called "The Cosmobreds." The painting was of a naked young man of a flying black horse, and according to the *Pictorial*, it was a departure from her usual work in animals and sailboats and portraits because "Mignon wanted to combine her love for horses and for flying." In back of the painting of the Cosmobred and Mrs. Gardner herself are some curtains, and if you ask me, they're the highlight of the photograph. They are plain white curtains, but the valances are covered with chintz daisies, and the curtains are trimmed, but heavily trimmed, with yellow and green pompons, the kind drum majorettes trim their skirts and boots with.

Inside the *Palm Beach Social Pictorial* are advertisements ("Dress up your diamond bracelet"), columns and pictures. The pictures show the people of Palm Beach eating lunch, wearing diamonds in the daytime, eating dinner, attending charity functions, and wearing party clothes. Most of the people are old, except that some of the women have young husbands. It is apparently all right to have a young husband if you are an old woman in Palm Beach, but not vice versa; in fact, the vice versa is one of the few things the columnists in the *Social Pictorial* get really upset about. Here, for instance, is columnist Doris Lilly writing about the guests at a recent party she attended: "Bill Carter (now U.N. ambassador to U.N.I.C.E.F.) proved he really does love children by bringing his latest airline hostess." And here from another columnist, Maria Durell Stone, is another guest list: "Then there were the Enrique Rousseaus, she's Lilly Pulitzer, and even Lilly's ex, Peter, was there with, well, as someone said, 'I don't think it's his daughter but she just might be.'" Every so often, the *Pictorial* prints pictures of people they describe as members of Palm Beach's Younger Set; they all look to be in their mid-forties.

There are two types of columnists who write for the *Pictorial*—locals, and correspondents from elsewhere. There are two advantages to being a correspondent from elsewhere: you don't have to spend the winter in Palm Beach, and you get a lofty title on the masthead. Wally Cedar, who writes from Beverly Hills and Acapulco, is the *Pictorial's* International Editor, and Liz Smith, who writes from New York, is the National Editor. With one exception—and I'll get to her in a minute: she's Maria Durell Stone—the local columnists in the *Pictorial* have tended to be relentlessly cheerful women whose only quibbles about life in Palm Beach have to do with things like the inefficiency of the streetlights on Worth Avenue. Cicely Dawson, who owns the *Pictorial* along with her husband Ed, whom she always refers to as "our better half," writes a goings-on-about-town column in which she manages to summon unending enthusiasm and exclamation points for boutiques, galleries, parties, and new savings banks in town. "Congratulations to Nan and James Egan of the James Beauty Salon on their recent twenty-fifth anniversary," Dawson once wrote. "No client would guess from the cheerful attitude of this wonderful couple what hardship they have had these past few months. After an illness-free life, James was diagnosed as having chronic kidney failure last December. Oh that Palm Beach County had an Artificial Kidney Center! . . . because that's what James needs."

In all fairness, Mrs. Dawson is almost a grouch in

comparison to Leone "Call Me the Pollyanna of Palm Beach" King, who until her retirement in 1973 could not find enough good things to say about the place. "Where else," Mrs. King once asked in a long series of rhetorical questions, "could you find families offering living quarters to people of low incomes, without at least making some sort of charge? . . . Where could you find friends with splendid flower gardens leaving a message with their gardeners to send certain people bouquets during the winter while they are off on a trip around the world? Where could you find big bags of fruit from a Palm Beach orange grove on your doorstep at regular intervals? . . . Don't let fabulously rich people throw you. They are just the same as anyone else except they can do what they jolly well please when they jolly well please. They have likes and dislikes, aches and pains, problems. They are just people."

Maria Durell Stone has left the *Palm Beach Social Pictorial*—she has been stolen away by the West Palm Beach daily paper—but her two years on the weekly coincided, and not coincidentally either, with what I think of as the *Pictorial*'s Golden Era, so I cannot leave her out of this. Mrs. Stone is a Latin-looking lady with a tremendous amount of jet-black hair who is divorced from architect Edward Durell Stone and has taken not one but two of his names along with her. She began writing for the *Pictorial* three years ago, and no one writing in any of the Palm Beach publications comes near her gift for telling it like it is. "I've done nothing but praise the Poinciana Club since it opened," she wrote last year, "but being a critic means that every now and then one must speak the truth and I am sorry to say it, but Bavarian Night there was a disaster."

Mrs. Stone's main problem in life—and the theme of her column too—had to do with being a single woman in a place where there are few eligible men. There are a lot of us with this problem, God knows, but she managed to be more in touch with it than anyone I know. Not a column passed without a pointed remark to remind the reader that this Mrs. Stone was looking for a Roman spring. "I met Vassili Lambrinos this week and he's divine," she wrote one week. "Dorothy Dodson, petite, refreshing and vivacious, gave a luncheon for him and I got to know him better—unfortunately not as much as I would like to, but what's a poor bachelor girl to do?" Another week, Mrs. Stone went to a charity auction: "There were numerous items to bid on and I did covet that stateroom for two on the S.S. *France,* but as luck would have it, someone else got it. I wouldn't have known who to take with me anyway, so it's probably just as well." Age was no barrier: "One of the best things of the evening," she wrote of the Boys' Club Dinner, "was the Boys' Club Chorus, which consisted of adorable little boys of unfortunate circumstances who sang many lively numbers at the top of their divine adolescent voices. It was heartwarming to hear." Apparently, Mrs. Stone's subtlety was not lost on her readers: "Stanton Griffis, that amazing ex-ambassador who sat next to me at the Salvation Army luncheon the other day, told me that if I really wanted to get the right man, I should put an ad in my column saying, 'Wanted: Intelligent, handsome, lean, tall, romantic type with kindness and money.' Well, now that I've said it, let's see if my octogenarian friend is right."

From time to time, something sneaks into the *Pictorial* that has to do with the outside world, and when it does, it is usually in Liz Smith's column. Miss Smith writes for the publication as if she were addressing a group of—well, a group of people who winter in Palm Beach. She interrupts her column of easygoing gossip and quotes to bring her readers little chautauquas; last year's were about Richard Nixon ("Hope all you people who couldn't stomach poor old Hubert are happy these days," one of them concluded) and this year's are about oil and the Middle East. ("So here are the most fascinating and frightening statistics I've read recently, from *The New Republic.* You remember *The New Republic*—it's liberal, left, and riddled with integrity, but even so, don't ignore the statistics.")

The rich are different from you and me; we all know that even if some of the people in Palm Beach don't. But it is impossible to read the *Social Pictorial* without suspecting that the rich in Palm Beach are even more different. One of my friends tells me that Palm Beach used to be a rather nice place and that now it's become a parody of itself; I don't know if she's right, but if she is, the *Social Pictorial* reflects this perfectly. If there were more communities like it, I don't think I would find the *Palm Beach Social Pictorial* so amusing. But there aren't, so I do.

The *Palm Beach Social Pictorial*, P.O. Box 591, Palm Beach, Florida. By subscription $10 a year.

*May, 1975*

# Brendan Gill
# and *The New Yorker*

Brendan Gill's *Here at The New Yorker* was issued to coincide exactly with the fiftieth anniversary of *The New Yorker* magazine, and, as such, it became The Event of the anniversary, an occasion for critics to pat the magazine on the back and, in addition, to undo some of the devastation that was heaped on it and its editor, William Shawn, some ten years ago, when Tom Wolfe took them all on in the *Herald Tribune*'s *New York* magazine. *The New Yorker* has come through this round with garlands, and so has Gill's book. It is a charming book, the critics say.

The people who work at *The New Yorker* do not think Brendan Gill's book is charming, but they try to be nice about it. The ethic of Nice is, in its way, as much an editorial principle at *The New Yorker* as the ethic of Mean is at *New York* magazine, and you can see, when you bring up the subject of Gill's book, that the people who work with Gill really want to be polite about it. What they generally say is that they would not object so much if only Gill had presented it simply as a memoir, or if he had made it clear that he knew nothing whatever about *The New Yorker* after the death of Harold Ross, or if he had managed not to publish it at a time calculated to cash in on the anniversary. Any of these things would help, they say. Well, I don't know that any of this would help. *Here at The New Yorker* seems to me one of the most offensive books I have read in a long time.

Brendan Gill is now sixty and went to work at the magazine in 1938, and someone I know there suggested to me that he arrived too late to understand its early years, and too soon to understand the late ones. That is unfair; the explanation for Gill's insensitivity probably lies more in his character than in bad timing. Gill's character is the shall-I-compare-me-to-a-summer's-day variety: he is a joyous, happy man, he tells us, who has never suffered a day's pain in his life. Compared to other *New Yorker* writers, whom he describes as unsociable moles, he is uncommonly gregarious and fun-loving. He attends five or six parties a week. "I am acquainted with far more people out in the world than anyone else on *The New Yorker,*" he writes. Life has been a lark. He was born into comparative wealth, went to Yale, made Skull and Bones (an achievement he mentions a half-dozen times), had a rich father to aid him in the purchases of his town houses and mansions and country homes, several of which are actually pictured in his book. The smug self-congratulation of all this extends to his professional achievements. "In sheer quantity of output—most trivial of measurements!—I am by now something of a nonpareil," he writes.

The book Gill has written is not really a book; it's a series of anecdotes star-dashed together at four hundred pages length, a sketchy memoir masquerading as history. The omissions in it are gigantic: there are bare mentions, captions really, of Lillian Ross, J. D. Salinger and Robert Benchley; on the other hand, there are oddly lengthy descriptions of pseudonymous minor writers and clerks who dressed badly, had oily hair, hung their wash in the men's room, committed suicide, or turned out to be homosexuals. The so-called younger writers at *The New Yorker* are virtually omitted. "I don't know the younger writers," Gill said recently, by way of explanation.

The people Gill does write about are a good deal less fortunate than the ones he omits. Part of the problem here is the form he has chosen; the anecdote is a particularly dehumanizing sort of descriptive narrative. But the main problem, once again, is Brendan

Gill. Most of the people he writes about are, for the most part, people he clearly thinks of as friends. God help them. The stories he tells, stories he seems to mean to be charming and affectionate, are condescending, snobbish and mean. Here, to take one interesting and subtle example, is Gill on cartoonist Alan Dunn and his wife Mary Petty: "[They] were cherished by their friends like prizes that had been won in some incomparable secret lottery; none of these friends wanted to risk making the Dunns known to the world at large, and the Dunns were content within their small circle and with the superb consolation of their work." Wolcott Gibbs, the subject of a long section in the book, was a man who we discover married beneath himself not once but twice, was rude, would like to have been tapped for Skull and Bones, wore a brown fedora with a tuxedo, smoked and drank too much, and "had as many affairs as the next man." And what of Gibbs's work? Gill tells us Gibbs was brilliant at parody, "a form favored by writers of the second or third rank," and then goes on to devote several pages to an analysis of Gibbs's only play, *A Season in the Sun*, which contained a character based on Harold Ross. The play, Gill tells us, was a waste of Gibbs's talents and was unfairly praised by the critics, who were fond of Gibbs. Stanley Edgar Hyman, another writer who had the bad luck to be Gill's friend, surfaces in his book to chase girls, wear multicolored socks with sandals, and drink himself into a stupor. He and his wife, writer Shirley Jackson, attend an anniversary party at the Gills' country home. "On a stretch of lawn between our house and the surrounding woods," Gill writes, "we had pitched an enormous white marquee; metal-lined boxes, ordinarily used to hold potted flowers, were filled with ice and scores of bottles of Piper-Heidsieck, and a very satisfactory occasion it turned out to be. . . . Shirley was wearing a shapeless, reddish coverall, which served to exaggerate her size and not, as she must have hoped, to diminish it, and with her sharp writer's eye she cannot have failed to note that to many of the other guests she seemed an apparition, impossible to account for in their world of strict bodily discipline."

I feel squeamish even quoting all this; it seems to me I am compounding Gill's cruelties by repeating them. I want to make one more point, though, before moving on to Shawn and Ross, and that is about Gill's prurience. Brendan Gill is uncommonly prurient, and his book is full of leering references to women, sex and adultery. Gill notes several times that he does not understand why his friends persist in thinking of him as a Catholic when he is in fact a *lapsed* Catholic; my guess is that they think of him this way because he is as prurient in person as he is in print.

Brendan Gill's book is dedicated to William Shawn, who has been *The New Yorker*'s editor since 1952, and he provides a number of anecdotes about Shawn that are meant to be jolly. They mainly concern Shawn's fear of automatic elevators and his extreme discomfort about sexual references. I cannot imagine that a man who is constitutionally incapable of taking an automatic elevator finds anything but pain in the situation; that does not seem to have occurred to Gill. He has even less comprehension of what Shawn has done for the magazine: there is only one reference in his book to *The New Yorker*'s coverage of Vietnam and Watergate.

It is generally accepted over at *The New Yorker* that Gill's greatest sin is in not understanding Shawn. I'm not even sure he understands Shawn's predecessor, Harold Ross. He paints him as a buffoon, a gat-toothed, ill-dressed social incompetent who made typographical errors and disdained Freud. All of this is doubtless true; but it is, like everything in Gill's book, only a small part of the picture. Shawn provided Gill with a seven-page essay on Ross that closes *Here at The New Yorker*. The essay tends to give Shawn's imprimatur to the book—it is said he regrets having done it. At the same time, though—and I have no idea whether it was intentional—Shawn's essay is a gentle but thorough rebuke to Gill: it has all the complexity and depth that Gill's book lacks. As Shawn writes of Ross: "He lent himself to anecdote. Because of this, and because his personal qualities were large in scale and included a formidable charm and magnetism, the serious and inspired work that he did as an editor tended at times to be lost sight of." The articles Ross published by Liebling, Mitchell, Bainbridge, McKelway, Hamburger . . . the list is endless, really, but the point is simply that *The New Yorker* has always published brilliant magazine writing; it has always been a serious publication—if not about its subjects, at least about its prose. Under Ross, the profiles had an edge and bite that have been sadly missing—and this is Shawn's weakness as an editor—in recent years. (In many ways, the war in Vietnam, and Shawn's decision to hammer at it, rescued the magazine from the blandness that still characterizes some of what it prints.)

Gill's *New Yorker*—under Shawn and Ross—is no more serious than Gill's view of life. It is a parody of *The New Yorker,* the Eustace Tilley stereotype, the frivolous, upper-class publication with a sensibility best described as Jaded Preppie, the old "Talk of the Town" column, we went to a party last night. Gill has written a history of the magazine to conform to his image of it. As he himself admits, albeit in another context: "I am always so ready to take a favorable view of my powers that even when I am caught out and made a fool of, I manage to twist this circumstance about until it becomes a proof of how exceptional I am. The ingenuities we practice in order to appear admirable to ourselves would suffice to invent the telephone twice over on a rainy summer morning."

*June, 1975*

# Bob Haldeman and CBS

The decision by CBS to pay H. R. Haldeman at least fifty thousand dollars to appear in the *60 Minutes* time slot this spring is one that no one at the network—no one with any sense, that is—defends any longer. Dick Salant, the head of CBS News, has gotten to the point where he admits flat out that it was a mistake. The news personnel were appalled at the decision in the first place, and when the interview turned out as it did, they began walking around with a smug sense of vindication. The only person I spoke to at the network who was willing to defend the action was the man who negotiated it, Bill Leonard, the head of something called soft news; and even his defense lacks conviction. It was worth doing, Leonard says, because it raised the question of whether the networks should pay former public officials for interviews. It's a shame CBS could not have managed to raise this question without Haldeman's help; Gordon Liddy, to whom CBS paid fifteen thousand dollars earlier this year, ought to have been enough. At the same time, though, I think there is something to be said for the Haldeman transaction: it was worth every penny simply because of what it demonstrated about television.

Television news coverage has gotten away with a great deal in recent years—partly because of its coverage of the Vietnam war. Television showed us the war. It showed us the war in a way that was—if you chose to watch television, at least—unavoidable. You could not turn the page. You could not even switch channels: all you got was another network showing you the war. All of us who had worked side by side over the years with television reporters, who had watched in dismay as the cameras moved in and the television reporter cornered the politician ("How do you feel about the vote, Senator?") or cornered the man on the stretcher being carried out of the burning building ("How do you feel about the fact that your legs were just blown off, sir?"), calmed down a bit during the war years. Television was showing us the war. But giving television points for that was a little like giving a hooker points for turning a trick; that, after all, is what television does: it shows things. And beyond that, television for the most part was showing us the war in much the same way it was showing us everything else. Simply, and in two-minute snippets. Bleeding babies and bleeding soldiers. Explosions. Helicopter insertions. GI's on stretchers being asked how they felt about the fact that their legs had just been blown off. We got very little from the Vietnamese: most Vietnamese do not speak English. We got very little about what the war was doing to Vietnam, about the corruption of the South Vietnamese government, its political prisoners, about the morale of ARVN, about the depth of racism among United States forces. There were exceptions to this, of course—documentaries, mostly, and here I think immediately of Robert Northshield's on mixed-race children in South Vietnam. But even documentaries were governed by the overriding fact of television: it is a performance medium. It must attract an audience. And the way to attract that audience, the people in television assumed, was to show the war in the most simple, sentimental way. Our boys. Dying children. And most recently, orphans. The condescension implicit in all this is obvious; what is not so obvious, I think, is the utter lack of thought among television people about how television *ought* to cover news.

I don't claim to know exactly how television ought to have handled H. R. Haldeman; what is clear, though, is that no one at the network ever considered doing anything but a traditional face-to-face interview. Haldeman approached Bill Leonard back in October, before the cover-up trial began. Through his lawyer, he submitted a handwritten outline for a book called *Inside the Nixon White House*, which an agent, Scott Meredith, had refused to handle. It is an astonishing document, amateurish and virtually puerile. "Richard Nixon led me," it begins, "into the four most satisfying, trying, productive, demanding, enjoyable, difficult, rewarding, challenging, stimulating—and truly whole—years of my life. . . . Nothing in the course of future events can change the facts or the goals, feelings and actions of those of us who proudly served a great man in a great time." The chapter outlines begin with short paragraphs of introductory remarks, followed by sections titled "Headlines," "Characters" and "Inside Stories." The introductory remarks to a chapter called "The Inner Circle" go like this: "Insightful anecdotes about the four key men—Kissinger, Connally, Mitchell and Ehrlichman—and other important men (Agnew, Rogers, Moynihan, Shultz and Burns) and groups of men and women (White House assistants, young staffers, Cabinet, Congress, personal friends and family) around the President, and their relations with Richard Nixon." The character list includes just about everyone who worked for Nixon, name after name, and the headlines, all properly capitalized, are: "Secret Nixon Plan To Make Connally VP"; "Martha Really Was the Reason Mitchell Quit"; "Kissinger's Salzburg Tantrum Was Just Latest in a Series."

Leonard and another CBS executive, Gordon Manning, went to Washington to discuss the proposal over dinner with Haldeman. "My conclusion," said Leonard, "was that there was a possibility it might be an interview of considerable lasting public value. I never did think he would say something on the air in terms of a holy confessional. He made that clear. But he ran the White House, and I thought if you could find out how he ran it . . ." Leonard paused. "Maybe I was a little naïve about that." The three men discussed where the interview was to be done, and who was to do it. (Leonard claims he thought of Mike Wallace from the first, which was logical: Wallace is a first-rate television interviewer, and he has always had good connections with the Nixon White House, which considered offering him Ron Ziegler's job in 1968.) All that remained to be worked out was the money. Haldeman's lawyer suggested a figure of either $150,000 or $200,000—Leonard, possibly from spending too much time around Haldeman, has suffered a memory loss about the exact figure. CBS said that was far too high. But they never attempted to call Haldeman's bluff by offering to put him on the air for nothing; they were, after all, doing him a favor. Instead, they settled on a price that was an incredible tactical error: CBS would pay Haldeman $25,000 *for each hour* of interview that was used. This was done, Salant says, to provide an incentive for Haldeman to be forthcoming, to be worth the money he was being paid. It did nothing of the kind. Haldeman managed to screw a television network in a way that eluded him in all his years of White House plotting against the media. (Haldeman also sold CBS twenty-five hours of home movies, of which the network used four minutes. Industry insiders suggest that Haldeman may have been paid additionally for the film.)

CBS never considered following Haldeman around for a couple of weeks with hand-held cameras in the hope that he might eventually reveal himself. They did not consider using Dan Rather, or any of the print journalists who knew enough about Watergate to interview Haldeman properly. They did not cut into the show some of the other television footage of Haldeman that was available, obtained at no cost, like the moment when he bared his teeth at the Ervin subcommittee; they did not contrast Haldeman's fuzzy, sugarcoated recollections with his remarks on the White House tapes. Instead, they sent in Wallace. Wallace does his homework. Wallace studies. Wallace was stuffed, like a Strasbourg goose, with papers and facts and questions and quotes. He spent fifty-five hours in preliminary talks with Haldeman—a period of time so long as to

make me suspect he left the fight in the locker room—
and when he sat down to tape, for over six hours, he
found out firsthand why H. R. Haldeman used to be
called the Berlin Wall. Haldeman gave a brilliant performance: he played the part of a vibrant football play-
er who had been taken out of the game by a fluke, a
minor muscle spasm no one could cure. I said only a
paragraph ago that Wallace is a first-rate television interviewer; that is what he is, and that is all he is. He
too gave a performance. He gave us a bit of obsequious-
ness, and he gave us a lot of exasperated sighs. And
two hours of sweet talk and exasperation did not make
up for the fact that Wallace just did not know enough
to follow through. Time after time, Haldeman made remarks that were not supported by the facts, and time
after time, Wallace blew it.

When Haldeman insisted that many of the ex-
cesses of the campaign were the fault of the Committee to Re-Elect the President, not the White House,
Wallace failed to point out that there was no real difference between the two, that Haldeman in fact controlled the CREEP secret fund. When Haldeman
claimed that Woodward and Bernstein had admitted
in their book they were wrong about him, Wallace
did not correct him; what Woodward and Bernstein
actually wrote was that they were wrong in saying that
Hugh Sloan had named Haldeman before the grand
jury as one of the men who controlled the fund. When
Haldeman made what was the only potential news of
the interview, by admitting that he occasionally chose
not to carry out Nixon's orders, Wallace did not press
him for an example not already publicly known; more
important, he neglected to ask Haldeman how, in view
of this, he could base his defense at the coverup trial
on the claim that he was just following orders. Haldeman's outline had made the CBS people believe that
he would be anecdotal and gossipy about the so-called
inner circle. But all Wallace got from him were the
headlines of his book. Secret Nixon Plan To Make Connally VP. Martha Really Was the Reason Mitchell

Quit. Kissinger's Salzburg Tantrum Was Just Latest in a Series. Wallace prodded Haldeman for embellishment, but to no avail.

Back in the days when it was still defending its decision, CBS claimed that it was paying not for hard news but for memoirs. Solzhenitsyn, Eisenhower, Lyndon Johnson and Walter Lippmann were also paid under this guideline. The other networks were swift—and hypocritical—in denouncing CBS. NBC, which paid Marina Oswald, Sirhan Sirhan, the Fischer quints, and recently negotiated a roundabout deal with John Dean, said through News President Richard C. Wald that they would never have done it. ABC, having paid Lieutenant William Calley indirectly for an interview, said through its News President William Sheehan: "A news maker should not be paid for an interview." CBS continued to insist for a time that it paid only for memoirs; in fact, the network paid Dispatch News Service and Seymour Hersh ten thousand dollars for an interview with Private Paul Meadlo on the My Lai massacre.

A few days after the second Haldeman interview appeared on the air, New York's WNET did a *Behind the Lines* show on the whole business, and on it, CBS's Bill Leonard asked a question. "If we could forget just a moment whether he was paid or not," Leonard asked, "was it in the nature of a public service? Was it important or not important? Was it useful or not useful . . . ?" It is an interesting question—largely because it is totally invalid. There is no way to forget that Haldeman was paid. He was paid. The smell of money perfumed both hours. The shows were dominated by the fee, and Haldeman's responses were dictated by how far he thought he had to go to earn it. And all in all, the entire episode has made me change my point of view on checkbook journalism. I used to think it was a mistake to pay anyone for a story. I used to think it made it impossible for serious journalists to cover events. I used to think it would mean that news stories would begin to go to the highest bidder. Now I think the networks should pay everyone. Hard news sources, soft news sources, everyone. It will serve to remind us that, at this point at least, there is no reason to confuse television news with journalism.

*July, 1975*

# The Making of
# Theodore H. White

He was alone, as always.

A man who finishes a book is always alone when he finishes it, and Theodore H. White was alone. It was a hot, muggy day in New York when he finished, or perhaps it was a cold, windy night; there is no way to be certain, although it is certain that Theodore H. White was certain of what the weather was like that day, or that night, because when Theodore H. White writes about things, he notices the weather, and he usually manages to get it into the first paragraph or first few pages of whatever he writes. "Hyannis Port sparkled in the sun that day, as did all New England" (*The Making of the President 1960*). "It was hot; the sun was blinding; there would be a moment of cool shade ahead under the overpass they were approaching" (*The Making of the President 1964*). "Thursday had been a cold day of drizzling rain in Manhattan, where Richard Nixon lived" (*The Making of the President 1968*). "I could see the fan of yellow water below shortly before the plane dipped into the overcast" (*The Making of the President 1972*). And now Theodore H. White looked at the opening line of his new book, *Breach of Faith:* "Wednesday dawned with an overcast in Washington—hot, sticky, threatening to rain—July 24th, 1974." It had worked before and it would work again.

White flicked a cigarette ash from his forty-sixth Marlboro of the day and took the last sheet of one hundred percent rag Strathmore parchment typing paper from his twenty-two-year-old IBM Executive typewriter. It was the 19,246,753rd piece of typing paper he had typed in his sixty years. He was tired. He was old and tired. He was also short. But mainly he was tired. He was tired of writing the same book over and over again. He was tired of being taken in, taken in by John F. Kennedy, Lyndon Johnson, Robert Kennedy, General Westmoreland, Richard Nixon, tired of being taken in by every major politician in the last sixteen years. He was tired of being hornswoggled by winners. He was tired of being made to look like an ass, tired of having to apologize in each successive book for the mistakes he had made in the one before. He was tired of being imitated by other journalists, and he was tired of rewriting their work, which had surpassed his own. He was tired of things going wrong, tired of being in the wrong place at the wrong time; the night of the Saturday Night Massacre, for example, he found himself not in the Oval Office but on vacation in the South of France, where he was reduced to hearing the news from his hotel maid. He was tired of describing the people he was writing about as tired.

We must understand how Theodore H. White got to be that way, how he got to be so old and so tired. We must understand how this man grew to have a respect and awe for the institutions of American government that was so overweening as to blind him to the weaknesses of the men who ran them. We must understand how he came to believe that all men in power— even base men—were essentially noble, and when they failed to be noble, it had merely to do with flaws, flaws that grew out of a massive confluence of forces, forces like PR, the burgeoning bureaucracy, television, manipulation and California. We must understand his associates, good men, tired men but good men, men he lunched with every week, men who worked at newsmagazines which had long since stopped printing run-on sentences with subordinate clauses attached to the end. And to understand what has happened to Theodore H. White, which is the story of this column, one would have to go back to earlier years, to the place where it all started.

*Time* magazine.

That was where it all started. At *Time* magazine. Not everything started at *Time* magazine—Theodore H. White developed his infuriating style of repeating phrases over and over again later in his life, after he had left *Time* magazine—but that is where most of it started. It was at *Time* magazine that White picked up the two overriding devices of newsmagazine writing. The first was a passion for tidbits, for small details, for color. President Kennedy liked to eat tomato soup with sour cream in it for lunch. Adlai Stevenson sunned himself in blue sneakers and blue shorts. Hubert Humphrey ate cheese sandwiches whenever he was in the midst of a crisis.

The second was omniscience, the omniscience that results when a writer has had a week, or a month, or a year to let events sift out, the kind of omniscience, in short, that owes so much to hindsight.

Until 1959, when Theodore H. White began work on the four-hundred-one-page, blue-bound *Making of the President 1960,* no reporter had written a book on a political campaign using these two devices. White did, and his book changed the way political campaigns were covered. He wrote the 1960 campaign as a national pageant, a novelistic struggle for power between two men. He wrote about what they wore and what they ate and what they said behind the scenes. He went to meetings other reporters did not even ask to attend; the participants at the meetings paid scant attention to him. And then, of course, the book was published, became a best seller, and everything began to change.

Change.

Change begins slowly, as it always does, and when it began, White was slow to notice it. He covered the 1964 campaign as he had covered the one before; he did not see that all the detail and color and tidbits and dialogue made no difference in that election; the political process was not working in the neat way it had worked four years before, with hard-fought primaries and nationally televised debates and a cliff-hanger vote;

the 1964 election was over before it even began. Then he came to 1968, and the change, mounting like an invisible landslide, intensified, owing to a massive confluence of factors. The first was the national press, which began to out-report him. The second was White himself. He no longer went to meetings where he was ignored; he was, after all, Theodore H. White, historian to American Presidential elections. Had he been a student of physics and the Heisenberg uncertainty principle, instead of a student of history and all the Cicero he could cram into his books, he might have understood what was happening. But he did not. The change, the invisible landslide of change, eluded him. He wrote a book about a new Nixon, an easier, more relaxed, more affable Nixon. He missed the point. He missed the point about Vietnam; he missed the point about the demonstrations. Larry O'Brien used to be important; now it was these kids; who the hell were these kids to come along and take politics away from Theodore H. White? He missed the point about the Nixon campaign too. And so, in 1969, came the first great humiliation. A young man named Joe McGinniss, a young man who had gone to low- and mid-level meetings of the Nixon campaign, where the participants had paid him scant attention, produced the campaign book of the year, *The Selling of the President,* and even knocked off Theodore H. White's title in the process. Then, before he knew it, it was 1972, another campaign, another election, and White went through it, like so many other reporters, ignoring Watergate; months later, as he was finishing the 1972 book, he was forced to deal with the escalating scandal; he stuck it in, a paragraph here, a paragraph there, a chapter to wrap it all up, all this sticking out like sore thumbs throughout the manuscript. That year, the best book on the campaign was written not by White but by Timothy Crouse, who had stayed at the fringes, reporting on the press. To make matters worse, Crouse's book, *The Boys on the Bus,* included a long, not entirely flattering section on Theodore H. White, a section in which White complained, almost bitterly, about the turn things had taken. He spoke of the night McGovern won the nomination in Miami:

"It's appalling what we've done to these guys," he told Crouse. "McGovern was like a fish in a goldfish bowl. There were three different network crews at different times. The still photographers kept coming in in groups of five. And there were at least six writers sitting in the corner—I don't even know their names. We're all sitting there watching him work on his acceptance speech, poor bastard. He tries to go into the bedroom with Fred Dutton to go over the list of Vice-Presidents, which would later turn out to be the fuckup of the century, of course, and all of us are observing him, taking notes like mad, getting all the little details. Which I think I invented as a method of reporting and which I now sincerely regret. If you write about this, say that I sincerely regret it. Who gives a fuck if the guy had milk and Total for breakfast?"

White sat in the Harvard chair given to him by the Harvard Alumni Association and looked with irritation at his new manuscript, *Breach of Faith*. Here it was 1975 and he had a new book coming out. What in Christ was he doing with a book coming out in 1975? He wasn't supposed to have to write the next one until 1977. Theodore H. White shook his close-cropped, black-haired head. It was these damned politicians. He'd spent the best years of his life trying to train these assholes, and they couldn't even stay in office the full four years.

White stared at the title. Breach of faith. The new book's thesis was that Richard Nixon had breached the faith of the American people in the Presidency; that was what had caused him to be driven from office. But deep down, Theodore H. White knew that the faith Nixon had breached had been his, Theodore H. White's. White was the only American left who still believed in the institution of the Presidency. Theodore H. White was depressed. Any day now, he might have to start work on the next book, on *The Making of the President*

*1976,* and where would he ever find a candidate who measured up to his own feelings about the United States and its institutions? The questions lay in his brain cells, growing like an invisible landslide, and suddenly Theodore H. White had the answer. He would have to run for President. That was the only way. That was the only way to be sure that the political processes would function the way he believed they ought to. That was the only way he could get all those behind-the-scenes meetings to function properly. That was the only way he could get all those other reporters out of his story. White realized that something very important was happening. And so he did what he always does when he realizes something very important is happening: he called the weather bureau.

It was forty-nine degrees and raining in Central Park.

*August, 1975*

# Richard Collin and the Spaghetti Recipe

It is generally agreed among the people who have any perspective on it at all—and there are only a handful who do—that the entire civic scandal of Richard Collin and the mysterious spaghetti sauce recipe could only have happened in New Orleans—which was, in fact, where it did happen—and for fairly obvious reasons. For one thing, New Orleans is one of the two most in-grown, self-obsessed little cities in the United States. (The other is San Francisco.) For another, people in New Orleans really care about food, care about it passionately, can spend hours arguing over whether Antoine's is better than Galatoire's or the other way around. What sets the people of New Orleans apart from the people of San Francisco in this respect is that in New Orleans, there is basically nothing to do but eat and then argue about it.

All of which should have made Richard Collin a welcome addition to the New Orleans food scene. Richard Collin is a restaurant critic. He is New Orleans's first and only serious restaurant critic. A professor of American history at the University of New Orleans, Collin, forty-three, began his career in food in 1970 as the author of *The New Orleans Underground Gourmet* (Simon and Schuster). A few months after its publication he was hired by the *New Orleans States-Item* to write a weekly restaurant column. In it, Collin employs an extremely elaborate system of stars and dots and parentheses and X's which takes over five column-inches of space to explain each week. In addition, he uses an expression he coined to describe things he particularly loves; he calls them platonic dishes. "This is my own personal accolade," Collin once explained. "The term is derived from Plato's *Republic*. It simply means the best imaginable realization of a particular dish." Collin's style of criticism can best be described as hyperbolic; it can also be described as self-important and long-winded. But he works hard, and his guidebook is considered as reliable as any city restaurant guide in the country.

In New Orleans, however, the question of whether Collin is reliable is not the point. The point is that he is critical—and in public. Arguing privately about the merits of various restaurants is one thing, but criticizing them publicly runs completely counter to the local spirit of boosterism. To make matters worse, Collin is not even from New Orleans; he is from Philadelphia and he is seen as an outsider who has stumbled onto a gold mine at the expense of local merchants. So when the episode of the spaghetti sauce recipe and the two thousand dollars surfaced a few months ago, the city fathers fell upon it as an excuse to ask the *States-Item* to investigate Collin. But I'm getting ahead of the story.

The position of restaurant cirtic is a new slot at most newspapers; nonetheless, the job has a tradition and a set of ethics. The classic American restaurant critic is rarely photographed, makes reservations under a pseudonym, cannot accept free meals, and never reveals his identity to a proprietor. Some restaurant critics have gone to extraordinary lengths to preserve their anonymity; last year, for example, Jack Shelton of *San Francisco* magazine was subpoenaed to testify in a local trial, and he appeared wearing a mask.

Prior to the publication of his book, Richard Collin followed traditional practices; in any case, it would have done him no good to reveal himself, since his name meant nothing. But the success of the book, the newspaper column (which ran a sketch of Collin alongside his by-line) and subsequent public appearances made Collin's face and name well-known. By

1973, when the revised edition of *The Underground Gourmet* was published, Collin had moved into a slightly revisionist phase of behavior. He continued to pay for his meals, but he admitted that from time to time a restaurateur managed to force a free one on him. He continued to reserve under a pseudonym, but it became increasingly difficult to keep from being recognized. He began to metamorphose into a role he thought of as kindly godfather, but which might more correctly be defined as participatory journalist. He became a close friend of Warren Le Ruth, whose restaurant, Le Ruth's, received Collin's highest rating: four stars and ten platonic dishes. He gave advice to owners and to chefs. He seemed to regard himself as an impresario who was going to bring to New Orleans cuisine the acclaim it deserved. "I frequently introduce myself *after* the check has been paid," he wrote, "especially in smaller restaurants that are doing well and that deserve to be encouraged. I also notify restaurants in advance when a favorable review is to appear in the Saturday paper so that the restaurant does not run out of food by six or seven in the evening, as has happened when the pending review was kept a secret. For this edition I have not been quite as anonymous as I was for the first edition. Many restaurateurs saw me on television or met me at speaking engagements around town. However, known or unknown, distant or friendly, I have continued to base my evaluations solely on the genuine merits of the food restaurants serve. I enjoy being a restaurant critic too much to allow my integrity to be compromised."

The trouble began in April, 1973, with what looked—to Richard Collin, at least—like a pure case of civic duty. Turci's Original Italian Restaurant was about to close. Turci's was a typical grubby neighborhood restaurant on Poydras Street in downtown New Orleans; it had sluggish service but a platonic spaghetti sauce. It also had a platonic veal parmigiana, but the important thing was the spaghetti sauce: it had a rich, tomatoey, almost burned flavor, and it was packed with meatballs, mushrooms and chicken. Collin had given the restaurant three stars and, with his customary enthusiasm, announced that Turci's cooking was "unsurpassed in New Orleans or in Italy itself." But times got hard for Turci's, the neighborhood changed, and Rose Turci Serwich, the daughter of the original owners, decided she would have to shut down. Collin heard the news and wrote a column suggesting that someone raise the money to move Turci's to a better location and save the restaurant.

A New Orleans businessman named Joe Bernstein read the article. Along with two partners, he had just bought a building on Magazine Street and was looking for a ground-floor tenant. Bernstein called one of his partners, Ben C. Toledano, who occasionally wrote book reviews for the *States-Item* and knew Collin; Toledano called Collin and asked him to serve as intermediary in arranging the purchase of Turci's. "It was an uncomfortable position," Collin recalled recently, "but it was part of my responsibility to the community at large." Collin went ahead and arranged for Turci's to sell its name and good will for a reported ten thousand dollars and for Mrs. Serwich to sign an employment contract. A year later, the new Turci's opened. It was beautiful. It was crowded. It was fashionable. And it was terrible. Everyone knew it—Joe Bernstein knew it and Mrs. Serwich knew it. Both of them were on the phone to Richard Collin to complain about restaurant personnel. Mrs. Serwich hated the chef. Mrs. Serwich had objections to the manager. Joe Bernstein was going crazy because of the tension between Mrs. Serwich and the chef and Mrs. Serwich and the manager. But most of all, there was the problem of the spaghetti sauce. "I couldn't go to a cocktail party or go out on the street without someone telling me the sauce just wasn't the same," Joe Bernstein recalled. "I became frantic." The problem with the spaghetti sauce was really a very simple one: there was no recipe for it, and there never had been. The old Turci's spaghetti sauce had been a concoction made of tomato paste and leftovers. The new Turci's had no leftovers, owing to a streamlined kitchen and cost accounting; the new chef had no idea what to do under the circumstances. In the midst of all this, Richard Collin dropped in to Turci's for dinner.

The next day, he called Bernstein and told him to come by his house immediately. Bernstein arrived within a few minutes, and the first thing Collin asked him to do was to sign a release absolving Collin of any responsibility for what he was about to say. Bernstein signed and Collin began talking. He told Bernstein to fix the spaghetti sauce, eliminate the crab claws from the menu, and do something about the chef, who, Collin said, was "a Massachusetts Greek who didn't know from Turci's." If Bernstein failed to make improvements, Collin said he would be forced to give the restaurant a bad review—which he had in fact already written, and he read a few sample sentences from a piece of paper: "Frankly, we would all have been better off last year had the real Turci's been allowed to die a natural though unwelcome death. . . . It seems to me that in the move uptown what the new Turci's has proven is that one can turn a silk purse into a sow's ear. Requiescat." Within a few days, the chef quit—Bernstein says it had nothing to do with Collin's ultimatum —and Collin returned to the restaurant for a review. He gave the new Turci's three stars. "Try finding the likes of Turci's even in Italy," he wrote. "The new Turci's has the setting this marvelous restaurant has always deserved—a splendid place in which to serve its grand food. . . ."

At this point, we must pause to introduce a new character in this drama, a person Collin refers to as "my own favorite platonic dish." Rima Drell Reck Collin is a professor of comparative literature at the University of New Orleans, an editor of *The Southern Review,* and, according to her husband, "the most creative and gifted cook in the world now." She had just finished writing a New Orleans cookbook with her husband and was planning to open a food consulting firm in partnership with Warren Le Ruth of four-star, ten-platonic-dish fame. "The firm," says Collin, "was an attempt to get her out from being Mrs. Underground Gourmet. She's got enormous talent, but in this town she is still Mrs. Underground Gourmet."

One day a few weeks after the good review appeared, Joe Bernstein visited Richard and Rima Collin to talk about the restaurant. He was still concerned about its inconsistency, particularly when it came to the spaghetti sauce. One thing led to another, and before the session was up, Bernstein had hired Mrs. Collin's firm to fix the sauce. Bernstein paid her two thousand dollars for two months' work—after which time she and Le Ruth, who had not been able to implement a new recipe, fought with each other and dissolved the partnership. The next month, Mrs. Collin sent Bernstein another bill, which Bernstein refused to pay. There was considerable shouting on Bernstein's part and considerable crying on Mrs. Collin's part. According to Bernstein, Mrs. Collin threatened his bookkeeper and said that if he did not pay up, the restaurant would be hurt. Bernstein did not pay.

It was at this point, Richard Collin says, that he realized for the first time that he was in a spot. "I was in a very bad situation," he said. "It was okay as far as helping the restaurant and shaking out the sauce—that struck me as a civic restoration—but once a falling-out occurred, I knew that anytime I changed the rating it would look suspect." In January, 1975, just before the Super Bowl, Collin nonetheless printed a revised set of ratings for New Orleans restaurants. Turci's was stripped down to an altogether new category—a star within parentheses, meaning "some good food but not a recommended restaurant." What intrigued the owners of Turci's about this new rating was that Collin had not eaten in Turci's at any time since his original review had appeared.

A month later, *Figaro*, a small New Orleans weekly newspaper (in which, in keeping with the tenor of this saga, Joe Bernstein's children own a minority interest), broke the story. *Figaro*'s editor, James Glassman, quoted Bernstein and Collin on the Turci's episode, and also quoted Chris Ansel, the owner of Christian's Restaurant, who said that Collin told him to fire his chef and cut down on the salt; when the chef failed to do so, Collin stripped Ansel of his stars and eleven platonic dishes. The *Figaro* article caused a sensation. The New Orleans Restaurant Association wrote the *States-Item* demanding that Collin be investigated. The Louisiana chefs association seconded the motion. A group of local restaurateurs tried to pressure the National Restaurant Association to drop Collin from a panel discussion at the association's annual convention. There were television debates. There was an acrimonious press conference. Mrs. Galatoire of Galatoire's accused Collin of not ordering a dish he subsequently reviewed. The *New Orleans Times-Picayune*—which has an active rivalry with the *States-Item* although both are owned by the Newhouse chain—unleased its food writer to attack Collin.

Eventually, of course, the furor died down. The editor of the *States-Item* admitted that Collin had been "indiscreet" and that some of his behavior bordered on "a conflict of interest." The *Times-Picayune* food writer announced that he would write a rival restaurant guide in which no restaurant would receive an unfavorable rating. Bernstein, not having managed to formulate the spaghetti sauce, moved on to specialize in canneloni. The people of New Orleans settled down to dinner. And Richard Collin learned a lesson. Not the exact lesson he might have—about the function of a critic, for example, or about the limits of critical involvement, or about the ethics of critical behavior—but he did learn something. "I learned," he said, "that restaurants have a limited life-span, and there's no point in trying to save them."

*September, 1975*

# How to Write a Newsmagazine Cover Story

## YOU TOO CAN BE A WRITER

You can learn, in your spare time, to write articles for publication, and if you master the art, you can be paid to do it on a full-time basis.

Of course, there are all sorts of writers. There are reporters, for example. Reporters have to learn how to uncover FACTS. This is very difficult to learn in your spare time. There are also serious journalists. But serious journalists have TALENT. There is no way to learn to have talent. There are also fiction writers. But fiction writers need IMAGINATION. Either you have imagination or you don't. You can't pick it up in a manual.

But there is one kind of writer you can learn to be and you will not need FACTS, TALENT or IMAGINATION. You can become a newsmagazine cover story writer. Just master the six rules enumerated below and you will know all you need to about how to write a newsmagazine cover story—or at least the kind of newsmagazine cover story dealing with life style, soft news, and cultural figures.

**RULE ONE: Find a subject too much has already been written about.**

To do this, read with care the following: *Women's Wear Daily*, *Vogue*, Joyce Haber's column, Suzy's column, the "Arts and Leisure" section of the Sunday *New York Times, Rolling Stone* and the movie grosses in *Variety*.

Any name mentioned more than four or five hundred times in the last year is a suitable subject for a newsmagazine cover.

**RULE TWO: Exaggerate the significance of the cover subject.**

Study the following examples to see how this is done by the experts:

"Today, a few weeks shy of twenty-six, Liza has evolved in her own right into a new Miss Show Biz, a dazzlingly assured and completely rounded performer. The Justice Department should investigate her. She is a mini-conglomerate, an entertainment monopoly" (*Time* on Liza Minnelli, February 28, 1972).

"At thirty-five, Coppola stands alone as a multiple movie talent: a director who can make the blockbuster success and the brilliant, 'personal' film" (*Newsweek* on Francis Ford Coppola, November 25, 1974).

"Finally, the film confirms that Robert Altman, the director of *Nashville,* is doing more original, serious —yet entertaining—work than anyone else in American movies" (*Newsweek* on *Nashville* and Robert Altman, June 30, 1975).

"At twenty-nine salty Lauren Hutton is America's most celebrated model of the moment—and the highest-paid in history, as well. . . . Her extraordinarily expressive face and throwaway sex appeal, captured in the strong, spirited photographs of Richard Avedon, have made Hutton a permanent fixture in the pages of *Vogue* and at least a passing fancy in five movies. And in contrast to the exotic stone-faced beauties of the 1960's, her natural gap-toothed, all-American good looks epitomize the thoroughly capable, canny, contemporary woman of the Seventies" (*Newsweek* on Lauren Hutton, August 26, 1974).

"Margaux is the American Sex Dream incarnate, a

prairie Valkyrie, six feet tall and one hundred thirty-eight pounds. . . . Effortlessly, Margaux stands out in a gallery of fresh young faces, newcomers who are making their names in modeling, movies, ballet and in the exacting art of simply living well. They add up to an exhilarating crop of new beauties who light up the landscape in the U.S. and abroad (*Time* on Margaux Hemingway and the New Beauties, June 16, 1975).

**RULE THREE: Find people who know the subject personally and whose careers are bound up with the subject's. Get these people to comment on the subject's significance.**

"Add to all this her beliefs in the trendy cults of mysticism and metaphysics and she becomes thoroughly modern Marisa, aptly crowned by the *International Herald Tribune*'s society chronicler Hebe Dorsey as 'the girl who has everything plus' " (*Newsweek* on Marisa Berenson, August 27, 1973).

" 'This event is the biggest thing of its kind in the history of show business,' modestly declared David Geffen, the thirty-year-old human dynamo, 'Record Executive of the Year,' chairman of the board of Elektra/Asylum Records, who just pulled off one of the great coups in the music business—signing Dylan away from Columbia Records" (*Newsweek* on Bob Dylan's concert tour, January 14, 1974).

"This is Roy Halston Frowick . . . known simply as Halston—the premier fashion designer of all America. . . . Halston's creative strength derives from personally dressing the most famous and fashionable women in the world, and while his name is not yet a household word, his impact on fashion trend setters is considerable. 'Halston is the hottest American designer of the moment,' says James Brady, the former publisher of *Women's Wear Daily* and now publisher of *Harper's Bazaar*. Fashion consultant Eleanor Lambert goes even further. 'Along with Yves St. Laurent,' says Miss Lambert, 'Halston is the most influential designer

—not only in America, but in the world' " (*Newsweek* on Halston, August 21, 1972).

**RULE FOUR: Try, insofar as it is possible, to imitate the style of press releases.**

"On the one hand she is very American, with deep roots in the South and an almost apple-pie adolescence (from cheerleader to campus queen). There is about her a touching innocence, openness, expansiveness and vulnerability. But at the same time she is no bright-eyed square. She breathes sophistication, elegance, grace, passion, experience. Dunaway has become more than a star—she is a style and a symbol" (*Newsweek* on Faye Dunaway, March 4, 1968).

"She is the rural neophyte waiting in a subway, a free spirit drinking Greek wine in the moonlight, an organic Earth Mother dispensing fresh bread and herb tea, and the reticent feminist who by trial and error has charted the male as well as the female ego" (*Time* on Joni Mitchell, December 16, 1974).

"There are many things gorgeous about Robert Redford. The shell, to begin with, is resplendent. The head is classically shaped, the features chiseled to an all-American handsomeness just rugged enough to avoid prettiness, the complexion weather-burnished to a reddish-gold, the body athletically muscled, the aura best described by one female fan who says: 'He gives you the feeling that even his sweat would smell good' " (*Newsweek* on Robert Redford, February 4, 1974).

**RULE FIVE: Use statistics wherever possible. Better yet, use statistics so mind boggling that no reader will bother to do simple arithmetic to determine their impossibility.**

One example will suffice here:

"[There are] one hundred million dogs and cats in the U.S. . . . Each day across the nation, dogs deposit an estimated four million tons of feces" (*Time* on the American Pet, December 23, 1974).

**RULE SIX: Study the examples.**

Read more newsmagazine cover stories.

Learn to use adjectives like "brilliant," "gorgeous," "original," "serious" and "dazzling" with devil-may-care abandon.

Learn to use clichés with devil-may-care abandon.

Master this technique and you too will be able to get a job writing back-of-the-book cover stories at a newsmagazine. You too will be able to take a subject, any subject, and hype it to the point where it bears no resemblance to reality. Whomever you write about will never be able to live up to what you write about him; but never mind. The important thing is that people will talk about YOUR STORY. They will talk about it for years. They will say how strange it was that the career of whomever you wrote about seemed somehow to slip after the cover *you wrote* appeared. They will allude ominously to the Newsmagazine Cover Curse. But you will know better.

So begin now, before it's too late. If it doesn't work out, you can always go work at a fan magazine.

*October, 1975*

# The Boston Photographs

"I made all kinds of pictures because I thought it would be a good rescue shot over the ladder . . . never dreamed it would be anything else. . . . I kept having to move around because of the light set. The sky was bright and they were in deep shadow. I was making pictures with a motor drive and he, the fire fighter, was reaching up and, I don't know, everything started falling. I followed the girl down taking pictures . . . I made three or four frames. I realized what was going on and I completely turned around, because I didn't want to see her hit."

You probably saw the photographs. In most newspapers, there were three of them. The first showed some people on a fire escape—a fireman, a woman and a child. The fireman had a nice strong jaw and looked very brave. The woman was holding the child. Smoke was pouring from the building behind them. A rescue ladder was approaching, just a few feet away, and the fireman had one arm around the woman and one arm reaching out toward the ladder. The second picture showed the fire escape slipping off the building. The child had fallen on the escape and seemed about to slide off the edge. The woman was grasping desperately at the legs of the fireman, who had managed to grab the ladder. The third picture showed the woman and child in midair, falling to the ground. Their arms and legs were outstretched, horribly distended. A potted plant was falling too. The caption said that the woman, Diana Bryant, nineteen, died in the fall. The child landed on the woman's body and lived.

The pictures were taken by Stanley Forman, thirty, of the *Boston Herald American*. He used a motor-driven Nikon F set at 1/250, f 5.6–8. Because of the motor, the camera can click off three frames a second. More than four hundred newspapers in the United States alone carried the photographs; the tear sheets from overseas are still coming in. The *New York Times* ran them on the first page of its second section; a paper in south Georgia gave them nineteen columns; the *Chicago Tribune,* the *Washington Post* and the *Washington Star* filled almost half their front pages, the *Star* under a somewhat redundant headline that read: SENSATIONAL PHOTOS OF RESCUE ATTEMPT THAT FAILED.

The photographs are indeed sensational. They are pictures of death in action, of that split second when luck runs out, and it is impossible to look at them without feeling their extraordinary impact and remembering, in an almost subconscious way, the morbid fantasy of falling, falling off a building, falling to one's death. Beyond that, the pictures are classics, old-fashioned but perfect examples of photojournalism at its most spectacular. They're throwbacks, really, fire pictures, 1930s tabloid shots; at the same time they're technically superb and thoroughly modern—the sequence could not have been taken at all until the development of the motor-driven camera some sixteen years ago.

Most newspaper editors anticipate some reader reaction to photographs like Forman's; even so, the response around the country was enormous, and almost all of it was negative. I have read hundreds of the letters that were printed in letters-to-the-editor sections, and they repeat the same points. "Invading the privacy of death." "Cheap sensationalism." "I thought I was reading the *National Enquirer.*" "Assigning the agony of a human being in terror of imminent death to the status of a side-show act." "A tawdry way to sell newspapers." The *Seattle Times* received sixty letters and calls; its managing editor even got a couple of them at home. A reader wrote the *Philadelphia Inquirer:* "*Jaws* and *Towering Inferno* are playing downtown; don't take business away from people who pay good money to advertise in your own paper." Another reader wrote the *Chicago Sun-Times:* "I shall try to hide my disappointment that Miss Bryant wasn't wearing a skirt when she fell to her death. You could have had some award-winning photographs of her underpants as her skirt billowed over her head, you voyeurs." Several newspaper editors wrote columns defending the pictures: Thomas Keevil of the *Costa Mesa* (California) *Daily Pilot* printed a ballot for readers to vote on whether they would have printed the pictures; Marshall L. Stone of Maine's *Bangor Daily News,* which refused to print the famous assassination picture of the Vietcong prisoner in Saigon, claimed that the Boston pictures showed the dangers of fire escapes and raised questions about slumlords. (The burning building was a five-story brick apartment house on Marlborough Street in the Back Bay section of Boston.)

For the last five years, the *Washington Post* has employed various journalists as ombudsmen, whose job is to monitor the paper on behalf of the public. The *Post's* current ombudsman is Charles Seib, former managing editor of the *Washington Star;* the day the Boston photographs appeared, the paper received over seventy calls in protest. As Seib later wrote in a column about the pictures, it was "the largest reaction to a published item that I have experienced in eight months as the *Post's* ombudsman. . . .

"In the *Post's* newsroom, on the other hand, I found no doubts, no second thoughts . . . the question was not whether they should be printed but how they should be displayed. When I talked to editors . . . they used words like 'interesting' and 'riveting' and 'gripping' to describe them. The pictures told something about life in the ghetto, they said (although the neighborhood where the tragedy occurred is not a ghetto, I am told). They dramatized the need to check on the safety of fire escapes. They dramatically conveyed something that had happened, and that is the business we're in. They were news. . . .

"Was publication of that [third] picture a bow

to the same taste for the morbidly sensational that makes gold mines of disaster movies? Most papers will not print the picture of a dead body except in the most unusual circumstances. Does the fact that the final picture was taken a millisecond before the young woman died make a difference? Most papers will not print a picture of a bare female breast. Is that a more inappropriate subject for display than the picture of a human being's last agonized instant of life?" Seib offered no answers to the questions he raised, but he went on to say that although as an editor he would probably have run the pictures, as a reader he was revolted by them.

In conclusion, Seib wrote: "Any editor who decided to print those pictures without giving at least a moment's thought to what purpose they served and what their effect was likely to be on the reader should ask another question: Have I become so preoccupied with manufacturing a product according to professional traditions and standards that I have forgotten about the consumer, the reader?"

It should be clear that the phone calls and letters and Seib's own reaction were occasioned by one factor alone: the death of the woman. Obviously, had she survived the fall, no one would have protested; the pictures would have had a completely different impact. Equally obviously, had the child died as well—or instead—Seib would undoubtedly have received ten times the phone calls he did. In each case, the pictures would have been exactly the same—only the captions, and thus the responses, would have been different.

But the questions Seib raises are worth discussing —though not exactly for the reasons he mentions. For it may be that the real lesson of the Boston photographs is not the danger that editors will be forgetful of reader reaction, but that they will continue to censor pictures of death precisely because of that reaction. The protests Seib fielded were really a variation on an old theme—and we saw plenty of it during the Nixon-Agnew years—the "Why doesn't the press print the good news?" argument. In this case, of course, the objections were all dressed up and cleverly disguised as righteous indignation about the privacy of death. This is a form of puritanism that is often justifiable; just as often it is merely puritanical.

Seib takes it for granted that the widespread though fairly recent newspaper policy against printing pictures of dead bodies is a sound one; I don't know that it makes any sense at all. I recognize that printing pictures of corpses raises all sorts of problems about taste and titillation and sensationalism; the fact is, however, that people die. Death happens to be one of life's main events. And it is irresponsible—and more than that, inaccurate—for newspapers to fail to show it, or to show it only when an astonishing set of photos comes in over the Associated Press wire. Most papers covering fatal automobile accidents will print pictures of mangled cars. But the significance of fatal automobile accidents is not that a great deal of steel is twisted but that people die. Why not show it? That's what accidents are about. Throughout the Vietnam war, editors were reluctant to print atrocity pictures. Why *not* print them? That's what that war was about. Murder victims are almost never photographed; they are granted their privacy. But their relatives are relentlessly pictured on their way in and out of hospitals and morgues and funerals.

I'm not advocating that newspapers print these things in order to teach their readers a lesson. The *Post* editors justified their printing of the Boston pictures with several arguments in that direction; every one of them is irrelevant. The pictures don't show anything about slum life; the incident could have happened anywhere, and it did. It is extremely unlikely that anyone who saw them rushed out and had his fire escape strengthened. And the pictures were not news—at least they were not national news. It is not news in Washington, or New York, or Los Angeles that a woman was killed in a Boston fire. The only newsworthy thing about the pictures is that they were taken. They deserve to be printed because they are great pictures, breathtaking pictures of something that happened. That they disturb readers is exactly as it should be: that's why photojournalism is often more powerful than written journalism.

*November, 1975*

# Barney Collier's Book

Barney Collier has written a book about Washington journalists, and the thing the Washington journalists in the book said to me when I called them up to say I was writing a column about it was: Don't; don't write anything about it; you'll just give the book publicity and end up selling copies of it. This is interesting, since it implies that these journalists believe that all publicity is good publicity, and if they believed that, none of them would be half as upset about the book as they are.

Nonetheless, it's a tricky problem.

Collier's book is called *Hope and Fear in Washington (The Early Seventies)*: *The Story of the Washington Press Corps*. The Dial Press is publishing it, and I'll get to them in a minute. The author, who is thirty-seven, was a reporter for the *New York Herald Tribune* and later for the *New York Times*. He left the *Times* in 1969 under murky circumstances—he was not fired, but it is clear that he was in some way made to feel that his presence in the newsroom was no longer desirable. A few years later, he published an article in the *New York Times Magazine* on columnist Joseph Alsop; subsequently, he was given $7,500 and a contract from the David McKay Company to write a book on Washington journalists. Because he was an old colleague, or a friend of a friend, the journalists he wanted to see gave him interviews; most reporters believe they have that obligation to other reporters. Because he was clearly down-and-out, they usually paid for lunch. Because he seemed a little strange—he did not take notes, and he asked odd questions like "What do you think of sex?" and "What is your definition of intelligence?" and "How much money do you make?"—most of them eventually stopped returning his phone calls. As Sally Quinn said to him at one point: "I get terrible vibes from you, and I don't know why."

Collier turned the book in to David McKay about two years ago, and it was rejected. His editor had expected a serious book on journalists and journalism; what Collier delivered, in the opinion of the publisher, was self-indulgent, inaccurate, impressionistic and libelous. "We felt," said a spokesman for McKay, "that it would have been immoral to publish it." The book was sent around to a number of other publishers— Collier claims that seventeen or eighteen of them turned it down, though his agent says that is a slight exaggeration. Finally, it came to rest at Dial, which paid ten thousand dollars for it. Dial felt the book would be controversial, and that it would sell. (I am continually fascinated at the difficulty intelligent people have in distinguishing what is controversial from what is merely offensive.) This faith was bolstered when material from the book on Sander Vanocur appeared in [MORE], the journalism review, and received more mail in protest than anything [MORE] had ever printed.

In his introduction to the book, Collier writes: "One of the ideas behind this book is that in order to more nearly understand the news from Washington you must more nearly understand the life of the person who tells you what the news may be." This is a valid proposition, and it might have made for a good book. It helps to know, for example, that Melvin Laird leaks to Evans and Novak when you read an Evans and Novak column saying that Gerald Ford is considering appointing Melvin Laird Vice-President. This sort of thing is not in Collier's book. Instead, the reader learns that Bob Novak has just given up smoking, and that Rowland Evans won't let Barney Collier see his tax return. (It's unfortunate that Evans did not: Collier might have discovered, in looking at it, how to spell Evans's first name.) Collier treats his subjects as celebrities. He writes about their marriages, hints leeringly at their infidelities, twists the quotes, jumbles the facts, misspells the names. He makes fun of what they order for lunch, how they eat it, and even that they paid his check. Nothing is off the record. "People tell you something and expect you to take care of them," Collier says. "They assume that off the record is everything you as a pal would leave out. It's a permeating thing in Washington." It is indeed permeating—and it's relevant when reporters end up taking care of someone like Henry Kissinger. But here it's ridiculous. Anyone who has ever done interviews knows how easy it is to make an interview subject sound foolish by quoting his casual conversation with a waiter, or by asking him asinine questions.

And that, of course, is precisely Collier's aim: to make his subjects look foolish. They have succeeded and he has failed; Collier's bitterness at the injustice of it all permeates everything he writes. It makes for an incredibly ugly book, which is in no way redeemed by the fact that Collier is open about his own life—his first marriage, his decision to give up his sons for adoption, his trials at the *Times,* and his travels in and out of sanity. The crack-up is one thing when Scott Fitzgerald writes it, and quite another when Barney Collier does.

But I wanted to write about Collier's book because it raises a couple of interesting questions. The first is about its publisher, and what I think of as the lie-down-with-dogs-get-up-with-fleas syndrome. The Dial Press sent Collier's book out with six jacket and publicity quotes. Two of them—from Sydney Gruson and Richard Goodwin—are accurate. Two others—from David Halberstam and Theodore H. White—were lifted from their letters to [*MORE*] objecting to the Vanocur piece; they were used without permission and referred only to the piece; Halberstam's quote is completely out of context. I spoke to Donna Schrader, publicity director at Dial, and Joyce Engelson, Collier's editor, and neither of them saw anything wrong with using the quotes.

Then there are quotes from Art Buchwald (". . . I came out good, but you better make sure the hood of your car is locked after the other people in the book read it!") and Helen Thomas ("I love it. I found myself going through all the emotions with it. I cried one minute and laughed the next. It's thrilling. It's spine-tingling. You got the people . . . just right . . . they all revealed themselves. It's really the anatomy of the press corps"). I called Buchwald and asked if he had given Collier that quote. "I didn't say that," Buchwald said. "He asked me for a quote, and I said, 'Weird.' 'That's it?' he said. 'That's it,' I said. 'Weird. *W-e-i-r-d.*' It's outrageous he's using something I didn't say."

I then called Helen Thomas, who had no idea she was being quoted at all. "I thought I was just talking to Barney," she said. "He gave me the book, and then he called to ask my opinion of it. I haven't really read it—I just went through it in a cursory fashion. If I wanted to put something in writing I would have done it myself. I didn't realize it was going to be used in that form. Life is difficult, to put it mildly."

"The first person I gave the manuscript to was Art Buchwald," Collier said when I asked him about all this. "I told him I needed a quote and that I didn't care if he liked it or hated it, but he could only read the book if he gave me a quote. My wife and I went to pick up the manuscript a couple of days later and I asked him if he would give me a quote. 'No,' he said, 'I'd like to get out of it. I don't want to be known as a collaborator.' 'Art,' I said, 'you made a promise.' 'Will you settle for one word?' he said. 'What's the word?' I said. 'Weird,' he said. We got up to go, and as we went out the door, he pointed to our car. 'That's a nice car,' he said. 'I came out good, but you better make sure the hood of your car is locked after the other people in the book read it.' "

"Did you ask him if you could use that quote?" I asked.

"Nope," said Collier. "He said I could use a quote, and he didn't make a beginning or an end to it."

Collier went on: "The second person I brought it to was Helen Thomas. I called her up afterward, and she said these things. She didn't put a beginning or an end on it, and she said I could quote her."

Collier sent both quotes off to Dial. Neither his editor nor the publicity director called Buchwald or Thomas to confirm the quotes; in fact, they seemed rather surprised when I suggested they might have done so. "I haven't followed this step by step," said Schrader. "I haven't looked at the material. We have six authors out on tour."

"This is the kind of book that obviously creates a sort of fuss," said Engelson. "The point of the book is that these people are public figures. A lot of the negative reaction to it came because of the article in [MORE], and a lot of that was people objecting to it because Sander Vanocur's wife was dying. It's certainly not Barney's responsibility that his wife, I forget her name, was dying. The timing had nothing to do with Barney. Mr. Buchwald is another set of fish. One day he says he said it. One day he says he didn't."

"What about the Helen Thomas quote?" I asked.

"I have it in writing from Helen Thomas," said Engelson.

"I don't think you do."

"I'm sure we do."

"I don't think so."

"Then Barney got it from her," said Engelson. "I don't see why she should object, anyway. It's a beautiful portrait of Helen Thomas."

I realized, as I read Collier's book, that I would not have been nearly as offended by it if it had been about movie stars—and that brings me to the second question it raises, about journalists and celebrity. In the past few years, journalists have indeed become celebrities; meanwhile, as if nothing had changed, they continue to parrot the old rule: "I'm a journalist, and I feel I have an obligation to give interviews to other journalists since I ask for them myself." Journalists may in fact have an obligation to help other journalists, particularly on substantive points, but they are under no obligation to promote themselves. And if they are going to—if they are going to behave like movie stars—eventually someone is going to come along and make fools of them. In some terrible way, the profession deserves the Collier book; it's the inevitable outcome of this daisy chain, this circle jerk of media interviewing media.

The logical ending for this column, I suppose, is for me to stop writing a media column. I'm part of the daisy chain. I stole one of the best lines in this column from Marty Nolan of the *Boston Globe*. I couldn't write this without the cooperation of other journalists. I really ought to give it up. I'm not going to, not yet.

But it's a tricky problem.

*January, 1976*

# The Assassination Reporters

Hugh Aynesworth and Bob Dudney work in a little office just off the city room of the *Dallas Times Herald* and things were running fairly normally there the day I dropped in to see them. A woman had just telephoned to say that she knew for a fact that Jack Ruby's brain had been controlled by a television station near the Dallas airport. The day before, a little man in high-topped sneakers had come by, whispered about some inside information he claimed to have, and finally confided that the Jews had killed President Kennedy.

Dudney, twenty-five, was in the eighth grade when John F. Kennedy was shot. He is new to the assassination beat, and he is still a little amazed by the people he meets on it. But Aynesworth, forty-four, has been covering the story on and off since November 22, 1963, and nothing fazes him anymore. "In 1963 only the most brazen kooks came out," he says, "but by the time Jim Garrison started in in 1966 and 1967, even the timid ones were getting into it. People want to be involved in this. I've heard five or six people confess that they were part of a conspiracy to kill Kennedy—only it turns out they were in jail, or in a loony bin in Atlanta, at the time. There were about five hundred people in Dealey Plaza that day. In twenty years, there'll be ten thousand."

The day of the assassination, Aynesworth was working as science and aviation editor of the *Dallas Morning News,* and he decided to walk over and have a look at the President's motorcade. He was standing catty-corner to the School Book Depository when he heard three shots. "I thought the first one was a motorcycle backfiring," he says, "but by the time I heard the second, I knew what it was. People started reacting in a very violent way. They threw their children down and started screaming. There was one big black woman who had been thrilled to death because she was wearing a pink dress the same color as Jackie Kennedy's. She threw up within five seconds of the shots."

After a while, Aynesworth saw a group of people running toward the Depository building. "On the fifth floor we saw three black guys pointing up to the sixth-floor window. There were FBI cars and a radio car. And then a funny thing happened. This shows what bad luck can do for you. There was a long-time police reporter for the *Dallas News* there named Jim Ewell. The FBI was working up floor by floor in the Depository building, and here comes a call over the radio: 'This is a citizen, an officer's been shot.' It was on Tenth Street, three or four miles away. I said to Ewell, 'You stay here, I'll go after that one.' He stayed, and of course he saw no one. I ran off with two TV guys and a Channel Eight news car, and we go to the Tippit killing. Then a call came in that there was something going on at the Texas Theater. I got there, and there was Jim Ewell, and I said, 'Jim, you take the upstairs and I'll take the downstairs.' Turned out Oswald was downstairs. I just got there in time. Oswald came up with his fist, which had a gun in it, and slugged McDonald, and the other cop jumped him from the back.

"Within a few minutes of that, I got a tip from someone at the police station about the two addresses in Oswald's wallet. We went tearing over to the Elsbeth address, where he wasn't living—I burst in on some wino and his girl shacked up together. Then we went to 1026 Beckley, where he actually lived. We were twenty minutes behind the FBI. There was that little old room, it couldn't have been more than eight by ten. The only thing they left in it was a banana peel.

"On Sunday morning, Jim Ewell had the assignment at the jail, but he got a flat tire on the way. I went over just to see what was going on and saw Ruby kill Oswald. It was pure luck that I saw it and he missed it all. He feels snakebit, I'm sure."

Today Jim Ewell is still a police reporter in Dallas, and Hugh Aynesworth—well, Aynesworth is still a reporter too, but he is also an odd sort of footnote to the assassination, the journalist who has spent more time on the story than any other. He is a walking compendium of names of FBI agents, New Orleans informers, assistant district attorneys, bus drivers and cabbies. He was the first reporter to print Oswald's diary and he sat shivah with Jack Ruby's family.

Aynesworth became so emotionally involved in the Clay Shaw trial that one of his dreams influenced the outcome of the case. "Suddenly one night I awakened out of a nightmare," he told James Kirkwood, author of *American Grotesque*. He had dreamed that District Attorney James Garrison produced a surprise witness who came in "and sat down and captivated the jury, winning the case hands down." He was so shaken by the dream that he wrote a letter to Shaw's lawyer, urging him to hire a private detective to investigate one of Garrison's witnesses, a dapper man named Charles Spiesel who claimed he had heard Shaw discuss the possibility of assassinating Kennedy. The detective discovered that Spiesel had filed a sixteen-million-dollar lawsuit charging the New York police and a psychiatrist with hypnotizing him and preventing him from having normal sexual relations; the information was crucial in discrediting Spiesel's testimony.

In some way, of course, Aynesworth is probably as addled about the assassination as some of the genuinely crazy people who come to see him. Unlike them, though—and unlike most of the buffs—he continues to believe that John F. Kennedy was killed by Lee Harvey Oswald, acting alone. "I sort of feel like a damn fool," he says. "There's nobody on earth who'd rather prove a conspiracy than me. I'd love to write it—if there was any damn thing that made me believe it." It's an odd

. . . . .ative reporters try to bring conspira-
. . . . . . . Aynesworth has spent much of his time
. . . . .em down.

". . . .et me tell you how the story about Oswald's
b. . . .g an FBI informer got started," he said. "There
was a note in Oswald's papers with the name James
Hosty on it. Hosty was an FBI agent, and in the beginning we thought Oswald was some kind of a spy or paid
informer. I worked the FBI stuff, and we'd run down
everything you could imagine. I even got Hosty's phone
records. I called the phone company and I just asked,
'How do you get phone records if you've moved?' I
never actually said I was Hosty—she just assumed I
was, and she sent them. Anyway, we couldn't put it
together except for these interviews where Hosty had
come to see Marina. And that's where Lonnie Hudkins
came along.

"Lonnie Hudkins was on the *Houston Post,* and
he'd been sent to Dallas to work on the story. He called
me up all the time, he would bug me and give me all
these tips that were nothing. I just didn't want him bug-
ging me anymore. So one day he called up and said,
'You hear anything about this FBI link with Oswald?'
I'd just about had it. I said to him, 'You got his payroll
number, don't you?' 'Yeah, yeah,' said Lonnie. I
reached over on my desk, and there was a Telex number
on a telegram, S. 172 I think it was, and I told it to
Lonnie. 'Yeah, yeah,' he said, 'that's it. That's the
same one I've got.' Lonnie could see the moon coming
out at high noon." The number eventually became part
of the lore of the assassination.

Aynesworth stayed on the *News* until 1966, did
some work for *Life,* and was on the staff of *Newsweek*
from 1967 to 1974. The story would die down for a
while and then crop up again. "Something was always
coming up," he said. "*Look* magazine bought the Man-
chester book, so *Life* felt it had to have something to
counteract it. They put an investigative team on it, and
in 1966 they were digging around. They moved to New
Orleans and worked with Garrison, did a lot of inves-

tigation for him. Jack Fincher, the San Francisco bureau chief, comes up with a little fag from New Orleans, a short-order cook who told him a story about Oswald and Ruby being seen in New Orleans as lovers, and then at the YMCA in Dallas. He wove a great tale. Fincher didn't know enough to know whether it was good, so they told him in New York to run it by Dallas and see what Hugh thinks.

"We got a motel room at the Executive Inn out by the airport, and we taped this story, and he really had it down. There was no way I could break him. I was beginning to wonder myself. He was going on and on, he'd seen them swimming, hugging and kissing, and he said they'd even tried to entice him. Finally, I looked at him and said, 'Wasn't that a terrible scar on Ruby's leg, that shark bite? Which leg was it on, anyway?' He said, 'It was the right leg.' He took a pause. 'No,' he said, 'it was the left leg. I remember now.' I said, 'You little son of a bitch, he didn't have a scar on his leg.' He started crying. I felt sorry for him— he'd been promised a good bit of money for his story."

Last year, after working a spell as a private investigator, Aynesworth joined the *Times Herald* and began working with Dudney. They make an interesting pair: Aynesworth is stocky and square, Dudney is lean and long-haired; Aynesworth is disorganized, Dudney is a compulsive file keeper; Aynesworth works the phone, Dudney writes. The *Times Herald,* under the by-line of its publisher Tom Johnson, broke the story last fall of the threatening letter Oswald wrote to the FBI prior to the assassination; Aynesworth and Dudney did much of the legwork and wrote the backup stories. Their biggest story, both agree, was a nonstory that took them weeks to put together. An FBI clerk named William Walter, who was working in the New Orleans office in 1963, told them that five days before the assassination he saw a Teletype saying there would be an assassination attempt in Dallas and that no one had done anything about it.

"When we first talked to him on the phone," Dudney said, "we were both extremely excited. The guy was very convincing."

"We interviewed him twenty-some times," said Aynesworth, "and we talked to everybody who ever knew him."

"We got flags everywhere," said Dudney.

"We gave him a polygraph," said Aynesworth, "and he didn't pass it."

"We never could get the one bit of information that proved it or disproved it," said Dudney.

"When we were three weeks into it," Aynesworth said, "CBS got onto it. Dan Rather called and asked me what I thought. I said, 'I'm ninety percent sure he's lying, but I'm not sure.' They did some film with him, chartered a plane to get it out, and once again Dan and I were back and forth on the phone. I gave him the results of the polygraph—with Walter's permission. Finally, CBS went with it—but in a very positive manner. So we came back with a detailed, massive study. Knocking these stories down is no good—but you have to do it. There's a lack of willingness in this business to say that nothing is there. Especially after a few bucks have been spent."

There is a reason there are only a handful of reporters working the Kennedy assassination—and that is that a lot of smart reporters have kept as far away from it as is possible. This is a story that begs for hundreds of investigators, subpoena power, forensics experts, grants of immunity; it's also a story that requires slogging through twenty-seven volumes of the Warren Commission report and dozens of books on the assassination. A lot of people are dead. Some of the ones who are alive have changed their stories. The whole thing is a mess. And while it's not likely that Aynesworth and Dudney will get to the bottom of it—that would be a little like shooting a bear with a BB gun—it's nice to know they are still down there in Dallas plugging away.

"The other night I was at a party," Bob Dudney said, "and we were talking about certain great events that shaped the lives of people my age. The emergence of the Beatles and the Vietnam war were obvious influences. And I said that I thought the assassination of Kennedy was a big influence—and as soon as I said it I corrected myself. Oswald's death was more an influence than Kennedy's. Had he lived, so much more would have come out. His death left us a legacy of suspicion and doubt that's turned in on everybody. It's unusual. Such a neurotic little man, who was really such a loser, you know, and he's left a very profound influence. The country would have recovered from the death of John Kennedy, but it hasn't recovered yet from the death of Lee Harvey Oswald and probably never will."

*February, 1976*

# The New Porn

Every so often, I manage to get through a day without reading the *New York Times*. This is an extremely risky thing to do—you never know whether the day you skip the *Times* will turn out to be the one day when some fascinating article will appear and leave you to spend the rest of your life explaining to friends who bring it up that you missed it. Fortunately, this rarely happens. But on Friday, November 14, 1975, I managed to miss the *New York Times,* and I learned my lesson.

That, as it happens, was the day the *Times* ran a page-one story by its food writer Craig Claiborne about a four-thousand-dollar meal he and his friend Pierre Franey ate at a Paris restaurant, and I think it is safe to say that no article the *Times* has printed in the last year has generated as much response. (The only recent exception that comes to mind is one that Charlotte Curtis wrote about cottage cheese.) In any case, a few days later, in desperation, I went back and read it. As you undoubtedly know, Claiborne had bid three hundred dollars in an auction for dinner for two at any restaurant in the world; because American Express was footing the bill, there was a stipulation that the restaurant be on the American Express card. Claiborne chose to dine at a chic spot on the Right Bank called Chez Denis, and there he and Franey managed to get through thirty-one courses and nine wines. Two things were immediately clear to me when I read the article: first, that the meal had been a real disappointment, though Craig only hinted at that with a few cutting remarks about the blandness of the sorrel soup and the nothingness of the sweetbread parfait; and second, that the *Times* had managed to give front-page play to a story that was essentially a gigantic publicity stunt for American Express. What good sports the people at American Express were about the entire episode! How jolly they were about paying the bill! "We were mildly astonished at first but now we're cheerful about it," a spokesman for the company said—and well he might have been. Four thousand dollars is a small price to pay for the amount of corporate good will the article generated—and that outraged me; I have dealt with the people at American Express about money on several occasions, and they have never been cheerful with *me*.

Because my outrage was confined to such a narrow part of the event, I was quite surprised a few days later when I began to read some of the letters the *Times* received about the dinner. There were eventually some five hundred in all, four to one against Claiborne, and the general tenor of them related to the total vulgarity of spending four thousand dollars on a dinner when millions were starving. Knee-jerk liberalism is apparently alive and well after all. There were references to Nero and Marie Antoinette, and there were also a few media-wise letter writers who chose to object not to the article itself but to the *Times*'s decision to run it on the front page. The *Times* printed a short and rather plaintive reply from Claiborne, who said that he could not see how anyone could claim that the meal had "deprived one human being of one mouthful of food."

All of this raised some interesting questions. For openers, how much money did Claiborne have to spend to cross the line into wretched excess? Would five hundred dollars have done it? A thousand dollars? Had he spent two thousand dollars, would the *Times* have received only three hundred letters? Would the objections have been even more intense if he had spent the four thousand dollars but put the tab on his expense account? Then, too, there is the question of editorial play: how much difference would it have made if the *Times* had run the article inside the newspaper?

These are obviously unanswerable, almost existential questions, and a bit frivolous to boot—but there is something more serious underlying this whole tempest.

Claiborne was clearly puzzled by the reaction to his piece. He had managed to commit a modern atrocity —even if he did rip off American Express, for which he is to be commended—and there is a good reason why it never crossed his mind that he was doing so: except for the price tag, what he did was no more vulgar and tasteless than what he and hundreds of other journalists do every day. Newspapers and magazines are glutted with recipes for truffle soufflés and nit-picking restaurant reviews and paeans to the joys of arugula. Which of us will ever forget the thrilling night that Gael Greene blew five hundred dollars on dinner at the Palace, or that spine-tingling afternoon when Craig and Pierre jumped into the car and drove all the way from East Hampton to Southampton just in time to find the only butcher on eastern Long Island with a pig's ear? Or was it pork fat for pâté? God knows what it was, but the point is that it should not have taken a four-thousand-dollar dinner at Chez Denis to remind the readers of the *Times* that Nero fiddled while Rome burned. All of this—let's face it—is pretty vulgar stuff. It's also fun to read. But when it's accompanied by a four-thousand-dollar price tag, it reminds people of something they should have known all along: it's not about food, it's about money. Craig Claiborne writes about consuming—which should not be confused with consumerism, or Ralph Nader, or anything of the sort. And in his way, he is representative of one of the major trends in publishing today; he is a purveyor of what I tend to think of as the new porn.

Before going further, I should define what I mean by porn in this context: it's anything people are ashamed of getting a kick out of. If you want to sell porn to a mass audience, you have to begin by packaging it in a way that's acceptable; you have to give people an excuse to buy it. *Playboy*'s Hugh Hefner was the first person in publishing to understand this; if he has done nothing else for American culture, he has given it two of the great lies of the twentieth century: "I buy it for the fiction" and "I buy it for the interview." Of late, Hefner has been hoist with his own petard. He has spent twenty years making the world safe for split beaver, and now he is surprised that magazines that print it are taking circulation away from his own.

The new porn has nothing to do with dirty pictures. It's simply about money. The new porn is the editorial basis for the rash of city and local magazines that have popped up around the country in the past ten years. Some of these magazines are first-rate—I am particularly partial to *Texas Monthly*—but generally they are to the traditional shelter magazines what *Playboy* is to *Hustler:* they have taken food and home furnishings and plant care and surrounded them up with just enough political and sociological reporting to give their readers an excuse to buy them. People who would not be caught dead subscribing to *House & Garden* subscribe to *New York* magazine. But whatever the quality, the serious articles in *New York* have nothing whatever to do with what that magazine is about. That magazine is about buying plants, and buying chairs, and buying pastrami sandwiches, and buying wine, and buying ice cream. It is, in short, about buying. And let's give credit where credit is due: with the possible exception of the Neiman-Marcus catalog, which is probably the granddaddy of this entire trend, no one does buying better than *New York* magazine.

In fact, all the objections the *Times* readers made to Claiborne's article can be applied to any one of the city and local magazines. How can you write about the perfect ice cream cone or the perfect diet cola or the perfect philodendron when millions of people have never seen a freezer, suffer from sugar deficiencies, and have no home to put potted plants in? How can you publish a magazine whose motto is essentially "Let them eat cheesecake"? Well, you can. And thousands of people will buy it. But don't make the mistake of giving the game away by going too far. Five extra pages on how to survive in a thirty-thousand-dollar living room, one extra price tax on a true nonessential, and your readers will write in to accuse you of terminal decadence. And when this happens, what will be truly shocking will not be the accusation—which will be dead on—but the fact that it took them so long to get the point.

Terminal decadence.

Exactly.

*March, 1976*

# Russell Baker

I have come to my devotion to the columns of Russell Baker later than most of the people I know, and I'm not sure whether this is because I am slow to catch on, or because Russell Baker is even better than he used to be. The answer, I suspect, is a little of both. In the last year, Baker has moved from Washington to New York, and the column he writes for the *New York Times* and its news service has shifted away from politics and toward urban life in general. I was about to go on to say something or other about that, but I realize that I have already begun to be unfair to Baker. Which is one of the problems of writing about him: as soon as you start to describe what he does, you do him an injustice. Urban life indeed. Baker did a column the other day that began with Franco dying and going straight to the New York Department of Motor Vehicles; it was brilliant, and there is no way to distill or describe it. You had to be there. And in any case, when I went to interview Baker and told him that column was a perfect description of urban life in New York, he assured me it was about urban life in Russia.

Baker is, of course, usually referred to as a humor columnist and usually lumped together with Art Buchwald, and that, too, is unfair. He is to Buchwald what Saul Steinberg is to Peter Arno: he tends to humor that is abstract, almost flaky, off the wall, cerebral, a bit surrealistic. He almost never writes a column that is a long joke; because of this, and because he builds on mood and nuance, a neat paragraph summary of a typical Baker column doesn't work at all. So I thought I would just go see him and let him talk, and the hell with anyone who wants a decent description of his writing. I should probably tell you that Baker is fifty, a tall, skinny man who looks a little like a hayseed. He is extremely low-key, terribly nice, and often seems on the verge of being embarrassed, particularly by praise of any sort.

Q: How did anyone at the *Times* know you would write a funny column?

BAKER: Nobody knew what the column was going to be. I didn't, the *Times* didn't. I was in the *Times* Washington bureau, and I had a reputation for being a "writer" in quotation marks—the quotation marks implied that there were reporters and then there were writers. I did a lot of feature-type stuff. There was no expectation that the column was supposed to be funny. I'd outlined what was essentially an idea for a casual essay column, the sort of thing *The New Yorker* had done in the late forties in "The Talk of the Town." The style would be casual, monosyllabic, simple sentences, small ideas. I did know at the outset that I was interested in the ironies of the public condition. I was fascinated by irony. But what you project on a piece of paper and what finally emerges are two wildly different things. When I sat down to write, what came out was what was in me. The first column ever printed was a spoof, a send-up of a Jack Kennedy press conference. Very quickly I began doing basic satires, traditional forms like dialogues, fantasies, hoaxes, parodies, burlesques.

Q: Was it difficult?

BAKER: At the start, yes. I didn't know what it was going to be. Now it has a rigid identity, and there are days when it writes itself. When you start a column, you're in a very creative state; you're building a personality in a piece of writing. It's a strange kind of business. After a while the column becomes a tyrant. You've created a personality that is one aspect of yourself, and it insists on your being true to it every time you sit down to write. As time passes and you change, you may become bored with that old personality. The problem then is how you escape the tyranny of it. In a way, it's always a struggle between you and this tyrant you've created that is a piece of yourself. In the last year I've gone back to the essay form and abandoned the satirical form.

Q: Is that because of moving to New York?

BAKER: I'm not so aware of that. The change is the subject matter. It's so easy to do Washington. You have nothing but subject matter. But what happens in New York? Who, after all, knows who Abe Beame is, or Hugh Carey? I've had to work a lot harder, to take special subject matter and make it mean something to people outside New York.

Q: Someone once said something to the effect that he'd never known a writer who had a happy childhood.

BAKER: I've had an unhappy life, thank God. I suspect all childhoods are unhappy. My father died when I was five—it's my first memory—and I was lugged off from Virginia to New Jersey to live with a brother of my mother. He was the only member of the family who was employed, and he was making thirty-five dollars a week. He was married to a lovely Irish-woman who ran the household. My mother had a job where she sewed smocks for twelve dollars a week, and I was raised in a matriarchy. I was imbued with the business that you've got to get ahead. I always had a job, an awful job, usually selling *Saturday Evening Posts*. I was just terrible at it. They'd open the door and I'd say, "Well, I guess you don't want to buy a *Saturday Evening Post*," and they'd slam the door in my face.

Q: How did you get into journalism?

BAKER: I'd always been a drifter. When I was at Johns Hopkins, I was the only guy on the campus who didn't know what he wanted to be. Everyone wanted to be a doctor or a scientist or an engineer. It was very depressing. In a vague way I wanted to be Ernest Hemingway—that was in the days when he was still read. There was a guy on the faculty who lectured on T. S. Eliot and also wrote for the *Sun,* and he told me about this job. I went to see the managing editor, and he offered me a job, and I thought, It's a good way to kill time until I get around to writing a novel someone can publish. It was 1947 and I did police reporting at night. I never went to the office, never wrote anything. I drifted from police station to police station, hung around hospitals listening to people die, and phoned in police-blotter stuff. I did that for two years. I was in love at the time; I was leading this strange upside-down existence, hanging out with raffish characters all night and sleeping till one or two in the afternoon. I kind of liked it. I was getting an education. But after a year, I decided to go ahead and write a novel. I spent a summer and wrote a ninety-thousand-word novel in three months. You know Capote's famous comment on Kerouac—"That's not writing, it's typing." That's what the novel was. I was a self-taught typist, and I was combining the typing exercises with the writing of a novel. It was very valuable to me later. I'm a very fast typist.

Q: And what happened to the novel?

BAKER: I shipped it around a few places and then I put it in the attic. It was about what it was like to be twenty-three years old. I discovered then that the world I was living in was so much more interesting than the world I was capable of conceiving. I was hooked on journalism. That was the end of it. I never went back to writing fiction.

Q: How did you get to the *Times?*

BAKER: The *Sun* sent me to London as its correspondent. I was twenty-seven, very young to be in London, but very adventurous. Things were very difficult in England then, and most of the American reporters went to the PX for food. I didn't. I lived like an Englishman off the English economy, and I lost a lot of weight. I was hungry all the time. I cut myself off from the American community. Most of the reporters hung around the foreign office to get the diplomatic poop. I felt the AP would provide that. I went to Parliament and wrote about the nature of British political debate. I wrote about what Sunday afternoon was like, and British eccentrics. I was really a kind of travel writer.

Everybody was writing about the British economy and taxes except me. So I began to attract some attention. Scotty Reston was head of the *Times* Washington bureau, and he wrote and asked me to come work there. I said no. I was happy—the *Sun* was about to bring me back to be White House correspondent, and that was my idea of paradise. I mean, what more was there? I came back, and after two weeks I realized I had made the worst decision of my life. I'd given up London for this pocket of tedium. I was sitting in this awful lobby waiting for Jim Hagerty to come out with a handout. At one point I was vacationing in Denver—when you covered Eisenhower you were always vacationing in Denver, writing stories on how many fish he had caught that day, or what he'd said at the first tee. Reston came through and offered me the job again. So I came to the *Times* on the condition I get off the White House. I went up to the Hill for a while, and the following year I was back at the White House. I got to Denver in time to cover Eisenhower's first heart attack. I handled the first Presidential bowel movement in the history of the *New York Times*.

Q: I read somewhere that you eventually became unhappy in the Washington bureau.

BAKER: I didn't have a period of unhappiness where I was unhappy with the *Times*. I was just at the end of my rope. It wasn't possible to deal with Washington in a very sophisticated way, and the *Times* was not a paper where you could be very creative or innovative. For a long time I was more than willing to trade all that for the education. It was the best graduate school of political science in the world. If you wanted to know what was going on in the Senate, you went up there and Everett Dirksen explained it to you. But I'd spent over seven years doing it. I knew the personalities. I knew what speeches they were going to make on any issue. I became restless. It was really a matter of discontent with myself—I knew the limitations of the *Times*. Then the editor of the *Sun* offered me a column, a blank check, really, any kind of column

I wanted. I thought, Yeah, that's what I want to do. It was a great out for me. There was an intimation it would lead to a bigger job at the *Sun*. We shook hands on it. I told Reston I was leaving and he was appalled. I was shocked that anybody cared. I went home and that night Orvil Dryfoos, the publisher, called and said, We're not going to let you leave the *Times,* and then they began making offers to me, and that's how the column began.

Q: And why did you decide to move to New York?

BAKER: Basically it was because a pipe burst in my home in Washington on a Saturday morning. I was very depressed. I suddenly realized I was going to have to put a lot more money into this house, and I said, "Let's sell the son of a bitch and get out of here."

*April, 1976*

# My Cousin Arthur Is Your Uncle Art

The other day, my sister Delia went up to the Bronx to buy a carpet from my cousin Arthur. I had last seen my cousin Arthur in 1963, when I went up to the Bronx to buy a carpet from my uncle Charlie, who is Cousin Arthur's father. Uncle Charlie and Cousin Arthur used to be in the carpet business together, but Cousin Arthur left the family business some years ago to go off on his own, largely because he did not get along with Cousin Norman, who was also in the family business and whom no one in the family gets along with except for Uncle Charlie, who gets along with everyone. Anyway, when my sister Delia came back from the Bronx, having bought a very nice carpet at a very good price, she called up.

"Guess who Cousin Arthur is?" she said.

"I give up," I said.

"Cousin Arthur is Uncle Art," she said.

Actually, as I later found out, Cousin Arthur is Uncle Art only some of the time; the rest of the time a person named Jeremiah Morris is Uncle Art, and that is part of the problem. Still, Cousin Arthur is Uncle Art more than Jeremiah Morris is Uncle Art, and if you don't know who Uncle Art is, that's either because you haven't had to buy a discount carpet in New York lately, or because you're not in the carpet business. Uncle Art is to the carpet business what Frank Perdue is to the chicken business: in short, he has his own commercial.

"My name is Art Ephron," read the first of Cousin Arthur's Uncle Art advertisements, which ran, along with a large picture of Cousin Arthur himself, in the *New York Daily News* in 1972, "and I've been in the carpet business for, oh, longer than I care to remember. And every few weeks it seemed one of my relatives would say, 'Uncle Art, I was wondering, well, uh, maybe you could get us a break on some carpet. You know, something *nice*. Cheap.' So, one night, I was thinking. If I could do this for my relatives, why not for everybody?" The ad went on at some length, spelling out the special things about Cousin Arthur's Redi-Cut Carpets outlets (coffee, no pushy salesmen, a money-back guarantee, free rug cutting), and it ended with what has become the chain's slogan: "It's like having an uncle in the carpet business."

I was so stunned to discover that one of those people you see pitching their products on late-night television was a relative of mine that I promptly went up to the Bronx to see Cousin Arthur for myself. I found him on Webster Avenue, at one of his stores, and he turned out to be an extremely affable man. He was also, incidentally, the largest Ephron I have ever met (he is six feet tall and weighs two hundred ten pounds) and the only member of the family I know of who has a beard (although I haven't seen my cousin Erwin lately, and for all I know he may have one too). In any event, we went out to lunch and he told me about his advertising campaign.

"I started this company in 1971," Cousin Arthur began. "I'd been living in Detroit, working in the carpet business, and I felt that carpet retailing was ripe for a plain, pipe-rack approach, sort of like Robert Hall. I'd had a run with regular carpet retailing. I'd worked for Korvettes. . . ."

"Is it true," I asked, "that E. J. Korvettes stands for Eight Jewish Korean War Veterans?"

"It's a base canard," said Cousin Arthur. "The 'E' is for Eugene Ferkauf, the 'J' is for Joe Zwillenberg, and Korvette is the name of a subchaser in World War Two. To get back to what I was saying, I thought there was room for a no-frills approach to carpet retailing with remnants, so I called my friend Lenny, and he found a location in Mount Vernon, and we opened up. We hired a small ad agency in Scarsdale, and they came up with an ad that read: 'Redi-Cut Carpets, a nice place to buy.' We stayed with them for about a year. The business was growing, but we weren't getting results from the ads. I'm a great advertising critic, but I can't create an ad from scratch. So I called Cousin Mike and asked him what to do." Cousin Michael Ephron is media director of Scali, McCabe, Sloves, the agency that created the Frank Perdue ad; he and Cousin Arthur had recently become friends on account of a carpet Michael needed for his den. "Michael didn't want the account for his agency," Arthur went on. "Big agencies hate handling retail ads. The detail work is incredible." Michael suggested that Arthur and his partner Len Stanger go see a small creative agency called Kurtz & Symon. "They made a presentation," said Arthur, "and we got married."

Kurtz & Symon went to work and came up with the Uncle Art ads; in addition, the agency had Uncle buttons printed for all the salesmen at Redi-Cut. Even Cousin Arthur's wife, Hazel, got a button that said Uncle Hazel. The ads worked. Pictures of Cousin Arthur as Uncle Art filled New York and Westchester County papers. Business got better. More branches were opened. And Kurtz & Symon began to press Cousin Arthur to take his advertising campaign to television. At the time, a man named Jerry Rosenberg, proprietor of J.G.E. Enterprises, a discount appliance store in Queens, had become a household word in New York because of his commercial, delivered in an unrelenting Brooklyn accent, that began: "So what's the story, Jerry?" It was logical for Cousin Arthur to go on television too. But it didn't work out that way.

"I got scared," said Cousin Arthur. "I'm no actor. I'm impatient. I'd gotten really annoyed with the amount of time it took just to do the print ads. They were doing these photo sessions of me where they roped off half the Mount Vernon store for two and a half hours just to take a picture. I was losing business. I was going crazy. And I didn't think I'd be any good on television. Lenny could have done it. Lenny's a real ham. Maybe the campaign should have been Uncle Len. But I didn't think I could do it. Suppose I blew it? So I said, Let's get a professional guy. They got an actor named Jeremiah Morris. Jerry's about five inches shorter than me, ten years older, he's bald and has no beard. Outside of that, he looks exactly like me."

Kurtz & Symon brought Morris and a toupee and a false beard up to the store to shoot the commercials. "I'm Uncle Art from Redi-Cut Carpets," Morris began, and Cousin Arthur became upset. He began to complain to both Don Kurtz and Jim Symon. "He kept trying to change the actor's performance," said Jim Symon, who I spoke to about all this. "Most of his complaints had to do with the fact that he, Arthur, was more handsome than the actor, and that he, Arthur, was taller. Then we showed him the ad when it was done and he complained some more. He said the actor was playing it too much like Jerry of J.G.E. By that time there was so much money committed to the ad it had to be run. It was an academic discussion."

A few weeks later, in the fall of 1973, the commercials went on the air. Cousin Arthur would sit in front of his television set, switching from one non-network channel to the next, watching Jeremiah Morris come on as Uncle Art six times a night. "I would look and listen and I would sort of resent the fact that he really didn't look or sound like me. It really began to bother me." Every so often, he would make his wife, Uncle Hazel, sit through yet another viewing of the commercial. "After it was over, I'd ask her, 'Do I really sound like that? Do I really look like that?' She'd say no. But everyone else thought I did. I began getting calls from people I'd known for years. 'I saw you on TV last night,' they'd say. No one ever said to me, 'Hey, that wasn't you.' Tell me. You've seen the commercial. Does that look like me? Does that sound like me?"

In fact, it doesn't. But in any case, the commercials worked. Soon there were four of them on television, and soon Cousin Arthur and his partner Lenny owned eight carpet outlets. Cousin Arthur could hardly complain. Or could he?

"There's something I think I should tell you," he said, lowering his voice so that no one in the Red Coach Grill at the Cross County Shopping Center could hear. "I think I'm getting a divorce from Kurtz and Symon."

"What?" I said.

"I'm thinking of dropping them and going absolutely gigantically big into radio."

"Why?"

"I spend thirty percent of my budget on agency fees," said Cousin Arthur. "On radio you spend nothing. The radio station writes the ad for you. And my selling will be done by disk jockeys like Bob Grant, William B. Williams and Julius LaRosa."

"But what will happen to Uncle Art?" I asked.

"That's a problem," said Cousin Arthur. "We may be at the crossroads for Uncle Art."

"Have you talked to Cousin Michael about all of this?" I asked.

"No," said Cousin Arthur.

"I think you should," I said. "I think what all this is really about is that you wish you'd done the commercial yourself."

"I do wish I'd done it," said Cousin Arthur. "I can't get angry at anyone about it, though. I could have done it. It was my fault I didn't. But you want to know a thing I really regret? I had a chance to be head of a giant record company once. That I really regret. For five hundred dollars I could have owned twenty-five percent of Elektra Records. You know why I didn't?"

"Why?"

"My father talked me out of it."

That didn't surprise me. Thirty years ago Cousin Arthur's father, who you may recall is my uncle Charlie, told my parents it was a good thing they were selling their house on Turtle Bay in Manhattan, because the United Nations was being built and property values in the neighborhood were going to drop.

Cousin Arthur shook his head. "I should have done the ad," he said. "It would have been a thrill to see myself on television. Let's be honest about it. Everyone wants to be recognized."

"But you *are* recognized," I said.

"Only by family and friends," said Cousin Arthur.

"That's not true," I said. "My sister Delia's cabdriver recognized you."

"What did he say?" said Cousin Arthur.

"He said, 'Isn't that guy on TV?' "

"That's what I mean," said Cousin Arthur. "That's not really being recognized."

*May, 1976*

# Daniel Schorr

At the CBS Washington bureau, they are trying to keep straight faces over what has happened to Daniel Schorr, but it's not easy. Schorr is not a popular man, and there are a lot of people who are thrilled that he has been caught committing the journalistic sins of coyness, egomania and self-service. These sins are, of course, common to all journalists, which is no excuse for getting caught at them. Nonetheless, his colleagues might have gritted their teeth and supported Schorr but for one thing: he panicked and attempted to shift the blame for what he had done, tried to implicate one of his co-workers in the deed, and that gave everyone the excuse they needed to abandon him entirely.

The issue of character probably should not intrude on a First Amendment case, but when it comes to Dan Schorr it's difficult to leave it out. Schorr insists that his problem ought to be shared by the journalistic community, that we must all hang together or we will most assuredly hang separately. As he put it recently: "It serves CBS, and it serves me, and it serves you—because whatever happens to me will someday happen to you—that we preserve a united front now. I really feel a little bit like the alliance in World War Two, where De Gaulle and Stalin and Roosevelt and Churchill sit down and say, You know, we're going to have some problems, but let's lick the Nazis first. . . ." This is an extremely peculiar metaphor, but the part that interests me is not the equation of Nazis with the House of Representatives but the phrase "whatever happens to me will someday happen to you." It is quite probable that what happened to Dan Schorr happened to him precisely because he was Dan Schorr.

There are elements of the story, in fact, that are reminiscent of *Appointment in Samarra,* or any novel the theme of which is that a man's character is his fate (or, put another way, that the chickens always come home to roost). The plot is a simple one: a reporter whose obsession with scoops occasionally leads him to make mistakes develops an obsession about a secret document and makes several terrible blunders that lead to his downfall. What happened to Dan Schorr is a real tragedy, but only because he did so much of it himself.

To recapitulate: Schorr, fifty-nine, a CBS reporter since 1953, managed to make a Xerox of the Pike Committee report on the CIA a few days before it was scheduled to be released. He broadcast several stories based on it. Then, a few days later, on January 29, the House of Representatives voted not to release the report. Schorr discovered he was the sole possessor of it, and set about getting it published, preferably in a paperback edition for which he would write an introduction. He asked his boss, CBS News head Richard Salant, whether any of CBS's publishing subsidiaries were interested and sent Salant a Xerox of the report. After a few days, Schorr realized that CBS was dragging its feet, so he contacted the Reporters Committee for Freedom of the Press. The committee put him in touch with its lawyer, Peter Tufo, who was also a board member of New York Magazine Company, which owns *The Village Voice.* Tufo and Schorr's business agent, Dick Leibner, struck out at two paperback houses—neither of CBS's publishing subsidiaries was contacted by them or Salant—and Tufo then made a deal with *New York* editor Clay Felker to publish the report. Felker agreed to make a voluntary contribution to the Reporters Committee, which he subsequently failed to do. In any case, the Reporters Committee had reversed ground and said it would not accept payment.

Schorr, meanwhile, had lost control. The report was about to be published in *The Village Voice,* which had recently printed an uncomplimentary article about

Schorr. For that reason, and to protect his source and himself, Schorr decided to abandon the idea of doing an introduction. "Once you start down a certain line," Schorr said later, "the steps by which one thing leads to another come very swiftly, and suddenly you're totally wrapped up in it. You want *your* copy published and not somebody else's. You find yourself saying, 'By God, I don't care if this appears in *Pravda* as long as it appears.' In the end you're amazed at how far you've come from what you originally wanted to do."

But what did Schorr originally want to do? These days, he says that his sole concern was getting the report out in public. "I had to consider whether I was going to cast the final decisive vote to suppress that report. . . . I would have been the one who prevented the American people from seeing a report that had been paid for with four hundred fifty thousand of their tax dollars." But that is only part of the story: Schorr was also concerned with getting the credit for his scoop. And he got his wish. On Wednesday, February 11, the report appeared in *The Village Voice,* with an introduction by *New York* writer Aaron Latham. On Thursday, February 12, Laurence Stern of the *Washington Post* published an article linking the report to Schorr. The *New York Times* denounced Schorr in an editorial, the House Committee on Ethics announced it would investigate him, and CBS suspended Schorr from his reporting duties.

The story so far is an exercise in bad judgment and bad form—neither of which ought to have cost Schorr the support of his colleagues. But it gets worse.

On January 29, the night the House voted to suppress the report, Schorr was at a reception at the Israeli embassy, where he saw his friend Harry Rosenfeld, the *Washington Post* national editor. Rosenfeld, whose paper had not been able to obtain access to the report, good-naturedly approached Schorr, grabbed him by the lapels and said, "I want that report." A conversation ensued. Schorr volunteered to write a series of articles for the *Post* based on the report. Rosenfeld said he was not interested, that he wanted his own reporters to see it. Schorr said he wanted the *Post* to print the entire text. Rosenfeld said he could make no such guarantee. Schorr said he could not do anything without consulting CBS. "Of course," said Rosenfeld. "The question is, are you through with it?" If Schorr and CBS were, said Rosenfeld, he would be glad to pay the cost of Xeroxing.

The next morning, Schorr saw *Washington Post* reporter Walter Pincus and told him that Rosenfeld had offered him money for the Pike report. Pincus reported the conversation to Rosenfeld who had already talked with two other *Post* editors, who thought any sort of arrangement with Schorr was a bad idea. He called Schorr and withdrew the request for the report; he also told Schorr he was outraged at what Schorr had told Pincus. "Schorr is a fucking liar," Rosenfeld said later. "We don't pay for news." For his part, Schorr claims he misunderstood Rosenfeld. "Somehow money was mentioned," he says. "Harry says he was only talking about the cost of Xeroxing the report. I don't know what that is supposed to mean. I had a Xerox machine and he has a Xerox machine."

The day *The Village Voice* appeared, Laurence Stern of the *Post* called Schorr and asked if he was the source of the report. Schorr was unprepared for the call. On the record, he denied that he had any connection with the *Voice*. Off the record, he conceded that he did have a copy of the report and had tried to get it published through the Reporters Committee, but he continued to deny responsibility for the *Voice* leak. "The last thought I would have would be Clay Felker," he said. Stern had independent confirmation that Schorr had provided the report to the *Voice* and went with his story. A few days later, though, when he was going through his notes of his telephone conversation with Schorr, he noticed a remark of Schorr's he had not paid much attention to at the time: "I thought I had the only copy," Schorr had told Stern, "but someone must have stolen it from under me."

The "someone" Daniel Schorr was trying to implicate at that shabby point was Lesley Stahl, a CBS reporter who is one of several CBS employees (along with Eric Sevareid, Phil Jones and Dan Rather) who do not get along with Schorr. The morning *The Village Voice* appeared, Schorr took it into the office of Washington bureau chief Sandy Socolow. This is Schorr's version of the story:

"*The Village Voice* came in on Wednesday. So I go into Sandy Socolow's office with it. I'm still in this funny inbetween stage. How do I tell CBS about my partners? How do I tell the *Washington Post* about my involvement? So here you have a day when CBS does not know it's me who's done this, and there is the Aaron Latham by-line. You have to understand that Aaron Latham is a boyfriend of Lesley Stahl's; he's a familiar figure around the office. Sandy looks at the by-line and says, 'Are you thinking what I'm thinking?' I shrugged. I did not say to him, 'You're off on a wrong tangent.' I did not at this point disabuse him. Then I heard Sandy asking one of the producers if he had been in the office when the thing was Xeroxed. I could see him formulating a theory that Lesley or Aaron had gotten hold of it in that way. None of this was said explicitly. The point is that there were a couple of hours when I did not dispel the suspicion. I couldn't have without saying it was me." Schorr paused.

"I think I went further," he said. "I had lunch with a junior Cronkite producer that day. 'What do you think of this report?' I said. I kind of led him to think that Lesley had something to do with it. I realized later in the afternoon that I was playing games for no reason at all. I went to Sandy and said, 'Before you start any investigation of the Xeroxing, I know Lesley had nothing to do with it.' I don't want to pretend I did anything particularly smart or wise. But if all this is blown up into a theory that I planned to blame Lesley or Aaron, it's just not true."

Sandy Socolow says that Schorr's version is "a fucking rearrangement of what happened of the worst sort. It is just an absolute rewrite of history. He came into my office that morning with *The Village Voice.* I had no reason to believe he was the source of the *Voice* story—he had hated the piece the *Voice* ran about him, and he'd stopped speaking to the woman who wrote it. He came in, and these aren't specific quotes, but he said to me, Shouldn't we check where Lesley and/or Aaron were while the Xeroxing was going on. The next morning the *Washington Post* article appeared, and Dan came in again and said, You have no reason to suspect Lesley or Aaron, and you can disregard everything I said to you yesterday." Don Bowers, the producer Schorr lunched with, called Lesley Stahl a few days later and told her that Schorr had flatly accused her of stealing the report from him. (Stahl consulted a lawyer about the possibility of a slander suit.)

There are a number of interesting peripheral issues here—the question of whether Schorr broke the ground rules in Xeroxing the report, the question of whether CBS or Schorr owned the report, the question of whether Peter Tufo informed Schorr of his conflict of interest—and I'm sorry I don't have the space to go into them. In any case, whether he had a right to or not, Schorr went ahead and bargained away a copy of the Pike report he had obtained as a CBS employee; that is the situation we're stuck with. I don't think CBS had the right to suspend him because he is the subject of an inquiry; they may have had the right to suspend him for not fully informing his employer that he intended to act as an agent for the report.

And so Dan Schorr is in what he calls "the full-time martyr business." He sees his lawyer, he speaks to college audiences, he picks up awards from the American Civil Liberties Union. And underneath it all, underneath this squalid episode, there is one thing that is crystal clear, and that is the legal question: whether the House of Representatives, having passed a resolution prohibiting publication of one of its reports, can then hold a citizen in contempt for causing that report to be published. The answer, for anyone who believes in the First Amendment, is that it cannot. It is impossible not to be angry with Dan Schorr for having made it so difficult for the rest of us to march in his parade.

*June, 1976*

# Upstairs, Downstairs

My friend Kenny does not feel as bad about the death of Hazel as I do. My friend Ann has been upset about it for days. My friend Martha is actually glad Hazel is dead. I cried when Hazel died, but only for a few seconds, partly because I wasn't at all surprised. About three months ago, someone told me she was going to die, and since then I have watched every show expecting it to be her last. Once she stuck her head into a dumbwaiter to get some food for James, who had finally recovered enough from his war injuries to have an appetite, and I was certain the dumbwaiter was going to crash onto her head and kill her instantly. Another time, when she and Lord Bellamy went to fetch James from a hospital in France (and Hazel and Georgina had a fight over whether he should be moved), I was sure the ambulance would crash on the way back. Hazel lived on, though, show after show, until there came the thirteenth episode. As soon as they mentioned the plague, I knew that would be it. It was. The particular plague Hazel died of was the Spanish influenza, which, according to Alistair Cooke, was the last true pandemic. I was sorry that Alistair Cooke had so much more to say about the plague than he did about the death of Hazel, but perhaps he has become wary of commenting on the show itself after everyone (including me) took offense at some of the things he had to say about George Sand.

Of course, Hazel should never have married James Bellamy in the first place. James is a big baby. Hazel should have married Lord Bellamy, which was impossible since Lady Marjorie had just gone down on the *Titanic*. Or she should have run off with the upwardly mobile air ace, which was impossible since he was killed on the very next show after she met him, along with Rose's fiancé, Gregory. (I never laid eyes on Gregory, but Kenny tells me he was a very interesting man, a natural radical, who met Rose by sitting on her cake.) Hazel's finest moment was the show when she met the ace, and they went dancing, and she wore a dress with tiny, delicate beaded straps, and turned out to have the most beautiful back I have ever seen. But other than her back, and her fling with the ace, and her occasional success in telling Hudson off, and her premature death, Hazel left something to be desired. Not as far as Ann is concerned, but certainly as far as Martha is concerned. "Let's face it," said Martha. "Hazel was a pill." In fairness, we might all be pills if we had had to spend our lives sitting on a chesterfield couch pouring tea, but that's no excuse, I suppose. Hazel *was* a pill (though not nearly as terrible a pill as Abigail Adams and her entire family), and she really ought to have married an older man who wanted nothing more than to go to bed early. Still, James had no cause to treat her so badly. Kenny is the only person I know who has a kind word to say for James, and here it is: "Somewhere there must be something good about him that we'll find out about eventually." Actually, James did have a couple of good weeks there, when he returned from the front to report the army was dropping like flies, but I am told by a reliable source that his behavior was derivative of Siegfried Sassoon, and in any case, he shortly thereafter reverted to type. The worst James ever treated Hazel—aside from when she was sick and dying of the plague and he was playing rummy with his father's new fiancée, the Scottish widow —was when she had her miscarriage, and he totally ignored her, and went off dancing with Cousin Georgina.

Which brings us to Cousin Georgina. Martha doesn't much like Georgina either. This puzzles me. I can understand not liking Hazel and liking Georgina, or not liking Georgina and liking Hazel, but not liking both of them? Georgina was a true ninny when she arrived in the Bellamy household, and she hung around with Daisy, who is the most unrelenting ninny in television history. (For example, when Rose found out that Gregory had left her twelve hundred pounds, Daisy said: "Some people have all the luck." I rest my case.) But Georgina has become a wonderful nurse, and I'm proud of her. Also, her face is even more beautiful than Hazel's back. As for the burning question preoccupying us all—will Georgina marry James now that Hazel is dead?—I say no. (Martha says yes.) Georgina sees through James. I know it. I see her marrying the one-armed officer she went off to Paris with, if only because she is the only person on the show saintly enough to marry a man with one arm. Ann, on the other hand, does not trust Georgina as far as she can spit. "I know she was a great nurse," says Ann, "but she reminds me of those bitchy women you went to college with who were great biology students. She has no heart." There is indeed some recent evidence pointing to Georgina's heartlessness: when Hazel died, she went off to a party. But the war was over, and who could blame her? I was far more shocked at the la-di-da way Lord Bellamy behaved; he got off an Alistair Cooke-like remark about the plague itself, and that was that. Only Rose was magnificent about it. Ann thinks the reason everyone (except Rose) behaved so unemotionally about Hazel's death was that she was a petit bourgeois and they had never accepted her. I disagree. I think it's possible that the same person who tipped me off about Hazel's death tipped off the Bellamy household, and they just weren't all that surprised when it finally happened.

Even Martha loves Rose. Rose reminds me, in some metaphysical way, of Loretta Haggers. She is so good, so honest, so pure, so straight and so plucky. Kenny worries that Rose is going to leave the show now that she has come into all this money, but I say she'll never leave: the actress who plays Rose created the show itself, so she'll never be got rid of. I sometimes wonder how they do get rid of people at that show.

They sank Lady Marjorie, I read somewhere, because the actress playing her wanted to take a vacation in Europe. But what about Hazel? Did they know all along? Did they hire her in the beginning and say, "Look here, Hazel, we'll carry you through World War One, but then you're through"? Or did they hire her planning to use her straight through the Depression? Did she do something to antagonize them? Did she know she was going to die, and if so, when?

We all know that Mrs. Bridges and Hudson are going to get married at the end of the next batch of episodes, which have already been shown in England. The reason we all know this is that the information was mentioned in the obituary of the actress who played Mrs. Bridges, who died of the flu in real life in Essex a couple of weeks before Hazel died of the flu on television in America. Was this planned too? Did they say to her, "Well, Mrs. Bridges, we'll give you a nice fat part for the entire series and marry you off to the butler in the end, but shortly thereafter you'll have to die"? I wonder. I also wonder how I'm going to feel about Mrs. Bridges and Hudson getting married. There's something a little too neat about it. Besides, Mrs. Bridges is a much better person than Hudson, who has become a mealy-mouthed hypocrite as well as a staunch defender of the British class system. All this would probably be all right and deliciously in character except that it is beginning to look as if Hudson is going to personify, in microcosm, the entire rise of Fascism in Europe. Ann is more concerned on this point than I am.

As for Edward and Daisy, they talk a lot about leaving the Bellamy household, but it is Kenny's theory that they are beginning to sound more and more like the three sisters and Moscow. Which is a shame, because I wish they would leave.

Here are some things we all agree on:

We are all terribly worried that Rose will never find a man.

We all miss Lady Marjorie a lot more than the

Bellamys do, and are extremely apprehensive about meeting the Scottish widow's children.

We all think the best show of the year was the one with the scene in the train station with the dying and wounded soldiers. The second-best show was the one in which Gregory and the ace died.

We would all like to know some of the technical details of the show—how the writers are picked, how much of the plot is planned ahead of time—but it is too dangerous to find out. Someone, in the course of giving out the information, might let slip a crucial turn of the plot. We would all rather die than know what is going to happen.

Mostly, we all wish *Upstairs, Downstairs* would last forever.

*July, 1976*

# Porter Goes to the Convention

Porter checked into his hotel on Sunday night and went to Madison Square Garden to pick up his credentials. He wasn't sure what he was going to need them for, since his story had fallen through. Porter was a reporter for the *Tulark Morning Herald* of Tulark, Idaho, and his editor had sent him to the Democratic convention to cover the mayor of Tulark, J. Neal Dudley, who was a delegate. "Just follow him around," said the editor. Porter had had big plans. He would follow Dudley to the Empire State Building and the Statue of Liberty. He would follow him into a taxi and they would have a funny experience with a New York cabdriver. He would follow him to Eighth Avenue, where J. Neal Dudley would be mugged while Porter looked on helplessly, taking notes. He would follow him to dinner at Windows on the World, where with any luck Dudley would be thrown out for wearing a leisure suit.

Porter had begun by following Dudley to the Boise airport and onto the plane to New York. After a couple of drinks, he asked Dudley what he planned to do at the convention.

"Fuck my eyes out," said Dudley, "and if I catch you within twenty feet of my room I'll kill you."

"I'm supposed to follow you around," said Porter.

"Make it up," said J. Neal Dudley.

Dudley got into a cab at Kennedy airport and vanished. Porter got onto the bus and rode to his hotel. It occurred to him that if he could just find J. Neal Dudley fucking his eyes out, he could bring down the administration of Tulark, Idaho, such as it was.

On the other hand, Porter had read enough articles

in journalism reviews to realize that he would have to find J. Neal Dudley in flagrante with a secretary who could not take shorthand and who had been flown into town on a ticket paid for with the proceeds from a secret sale of Tulark municipal bonds. Otherwise, his editor would refuse to print the story on the grounds that it was an invasion of J. Neal Dudley's privacy and a surefire way for the paper to lose the advertising from J. Neal Dudley's appliance dealership.

Porter decided to forget it. He would make the story up. He could always talk to enough delegates to put something together about what J. Neal Dudley would have done at the convention had he actually attended it.

So after getting his credentials, Porter set out to find a delegate. He went to the Statler Hilton lobby and spotted a large man wearing a ridiculous hat. Porter approached him.

"Porter of the *Tulark Morning Herald,*" he said.

"Ken Franklin of *Newsday,*" said the man in the hat. "Can I interview you?"

"I beg your pardon?" said Porter.

Franklin explained that he was the media reporter for *Newsday* and he just wanted to ask Porter the questions he'd been asking other reporters.

"Sure," said Porter. "Shoot."

"What are you planning to write about?" asked Franklin.

"I don't know," said Porter.

"That's what they all say," said Franklin. "There are twice as many media people here as delegates, and there's no story."

"There's no story?" said Porter.

"That's what they all say," said Franklin.

"What else do they all say?" said Porter.

"They all say that because there's no news story, there are no feature stories either."

"What about the hookers?" said Porter.

"All the hookers are taken," said Franklin. "The

*New York Post* signed them all to exclusive contracts last week."

Porter bought himself a beer in the bar and looked around. He spotted a man wearing delegate's credentials and went over to him.

"Porter of the *Tulark Morning Herald*," he said.

"Suzanne Cox of the *Chicago Tribune*," said the woman sitting next to the delegate. "Get lost. This one's mine for the week."

"Could I ask *you* a question?" Porter said to Suzanne Cox.

"No, you can't," said a small boy next to Miss Cox.

"Who are you?" asked Porter.

"Brian Finley," said the boy. "I'm a reporter from *Children's Express*, and *I'm* covering *her*."

"Who's covering you?" asked Porter.

"Scotty Reston," said Brian Finley, "but he's gone to the men's room."

"I see," said Porter and went back to the bar.

"Jarvis of *Time* magazine," said a voice behind him. He turned around. Jarvis of *Time* magazine was very pretty. She was also a media reporter.

"Porter of the *Tulark Morning Herald*," Porter said. "I don't know what I'm writing about. There's no story. Because there's no news story, there are no feature stories either."

"What about the hookers?" said Jarvis.

"The hookers are taken," said Porter.

"Oh, God," said Jarvis. "I wonder if my writer knows that."

"Your writer?" said Porter, but Jarvis had rushed out of the bar.

Monday night Porter got a floor pass and watched Sally Quinn and Ben Bradlee being photographed. Then he joined a large crowd that was watching in disbelief as Evans and Novak had a conversation with each other. In the distance, Porter could hear Barbara Jordan speaking, but just barely. He wished he had stayed in his room and watched the convention on television. When the session ended, he bumped into Ken Franklin from *Newsday*.

"What are you writing about?" asked Franklin.

"I don't know," said Porter.

"Nobody's saying that today," said Franklin. "Today people have figured out what they're doing."

"Not me," said Porter.

Franklin took Porter to the *Rolling Stone* party that night. When they arrived, several hundred people on the street were pushing up against the door to the party, and several dozen police were trying to hold them back.

"Who's that with Seymour Hersh?" someone asked.

"Paul Newman," someone answered.

Porter managed to push his way up to the front door, but it was locked. Every so often, a man would appear at the door and point out someone in the crowd and the police would scoop up the someone and get him through the door. Porter squeezed in with Walter Cronkite's entourage, but once inside he found that the only topic of conversation was what was going on outside. A large group of people upstairs were watching a television monitor showing pictures of the scene on the street, and another large group of people were watching themselves on a public-access television channel.

"Porter of the *Tulark Morning Herald*!" a voice shouted.

Porter looked around. It was Jarvis of *Time* magazine.

"What are you doing?" she said.

"Leaving," he said. "Do you want to come?"

"Yes," said Jarvis.

Later, in Porter's hotel room, Jarvis began to undress. "I hope this is off the record," she said.

"Likewise," said Porter.

At that moment, the phone rang.

"Porter of the *Tulark Morning Herald*," said Porter.

"This is the New York City police," said a man on the phone. "We picked up a naked man dancing on Thirty-sixth Street. He says he's the mayor of Tulark, Idaho. Your name was in his pocket."

"Is he with his secretary?" asked Porter.

"Yes," said the policeman.

"Was she flown here on city money?" asked Porter.

"Yes," said the policeman.

"Can she take shorthand?"

"No," said the policeman.

"I'll be right there," said Porter. He put down the phone and started to dress. "I'm sorry, Jarvis," he said. "I have to go out to become a media star."

"That's all right," said Jarvis. "I can wait."

*October, 1976*

# Gentlemen's Agreement

*Esquire* refused to run this column. It was printed in [*MORE*], the journalism review.

In November, 1975, *Esquire* magazine published an article by a young writer named Bo Burlingham. It was called "The Other Tricky Dick," and it was a long reporting piece, ten thousand words or so, on Richard Goodwin, author, speechwriter to Presidents, and then-fiancé of Lyndon Johnson's biographer Doris Kearns. I was the editor on the piece. Burlingham portrayed Goodwin as an ambitious, crafty manipulator, a brilliant man who loved to outsmart his friends and associates to further his career. The article was carefully reported, the facts in it checked by the magazine's research department, and *Esquire*'s lawyer and managing editor grilled Burlingham on his sources for the article. All of us on the editorial side of the magazine believe that Burlingham's article was solid. Which does not explain how it came to pass that a few weeks ago, Esquire, Inc., decided to pay Goodwin $12,500 and to print the apologetic column about the article which appears in the November issue.

Magazines settle libel suits out of court all the time, of course. Not all magazines—*The New Yorker* has a strict policy against it; but many other magazines believe that it is cheaper to settle than to pay the high costs of litigation. At *Playboy,* I'm told, they say that they have never lost a libel case; the reason is that the magazine settles before it gets to court. All of this is a fairly well-kept secret in the magazine business; in fact, one of the arguments put to me against my writing this column was that if it becomes known that *Esquire* settles out of court, every joker whose name is mentioned in the magazine might end up suing. I rather doubt that will happen—but in any case, my concern is not with future nuisance suits, merely with this one.

The trouble with Goodwin began in August, 1975, before Burlingham's article even appeared in the magazine. Doris Kearns, who is now Goodwin's wife, came to New York to see me and Don Erickson, editor of *Esquire*. She asked us to kill the article. She said that Goodwin had become so nervous about what it might contain that he had taken to his bed on Cape Cod and had been there for two weeks. At that point, the article was on the presses and could not have been killed if Richard Goodwin dropped dead. We told her this. Then, a few days before publication, a telegram arrived—I can't remember whether it was from Goodwin or from a friend of Goodwin—putting the magazine on some sort of legal notice. A rumor came floating through that Goodwin had hired President Nixon's former lawyer James St. Clair and was planning to sue *Esquire* for libel. Then nothing for a while.

In the early months of 1976—I'm sorry to be so fuzzy about dates, but I didn't know what was going on—a man named Arnold Hyatt telephoned the president of Esquire, Inc., A. L. Blinder. Hyatt, a Boston shoe manufacturer and contributor to Democratic campaigns, knew both Blinder and Goodwin, and he apparently suggested the two men get together and work this thing out like gentlemen. A couple of points about Abe Blinder. The first is that a few years ago, he and the rest of the magazine's management were slightly traumatized by the result of a lawsuit William F. Buckley filed against *Esquire* over an article by Gore Vidal. *Esquire*'s lawyers wanted to fight the suit; they were certain it would be dismissed in a summary judgment. But it wasn't, and the ultimate cost to the company, including the eventual out-of-court settlement, was in the neighborhood of $350,000. A second point is that Blinder takes pride in the fact that he rarely interferes in the magazine's editorial matters. When I interviewed him about the Goodwin matter, he told me that he probably would not allow this column to be printed in the magazine—but he added that he had vetoed only one other article in his thirty-three-year history at *Esquire*. "It was about Morris Lapidus, the architect of the Fontainebleau Hotel," he said, "and it was very negative, very uncomplimentary. The Tisch brothers are good friends of mine, and they called and told me it would be bad for the hotel business if we printed it."

After Hyatt's call, Blinder spoke to Goodwin and arranged a lunch for himself, Goodwin, Kearns and Arnold Gingrich, the editor in chief and founder of *Esquire*. Goodwin arrived at the lunch with a set of papers containing a legal complaint and an itemization of grievances against the article. Blinder told Goodwin he had three alternatives: he could write a letter to the editor, he could sue, or he could forget it. Goodwin said that a letter to the editor would simply be his word against Burlingham's. But he indicated that he would be willing to work something out short of a lawsuit. At this point, Arnold Gingrich made a suggestion. He wrote a monthly column in which he often commented on articles in the magazine, and he might be able to write something that would reflect Goodwin's version of events. A token payment of one thousand dollars was mentioned, and everyone went home. A few weeks later, Goodwin met with Gingrich to draft the column. The next day, Gingrich was hospitalized with lung cancer; he died in July.

While Gingrich was ill, the column that appears in this issue was written by Don Erickson, now editor in chief of the magazine. In it, Gingrich relates that after reading Burlingham's article, which portrayed Goodwin as a Sammy Glick, he was surprised to meet Goodwin and find no trace at all of the ruthlessness Burlingham alluded to. Burlingham's portrait, said Gingrich, "is sufficiently at odds with the man himself that an appraisal is in order. . . . The piece made him out to be a guy who didn't pay his debts. But what we didn't say was that he had never had his credit withdrawn anywhere and that, with his holdings in Maine, he has assets several times his liabilities. And we made him out to be a man who goes around scaring people, including women, with guns. We didn't report that his gun hobby has never gone further than shooting at small birds and clay pigeons. He never owned a handgun, he told me. The one we reported on turned out to be a toy belonging to his son, he said. We implied that he had a streak of kleptomania and produced an incident that didn't prove it."

As it continues, the column is extremely clever. It is framed as one man's opinion, not as a formal apology, so there was no need for the magazine to show it to the author or editor involved. It is full of "he said" and "he told me," so that nothing is actually denied; still, the impression is that there was somehow faulty, incomplete or inaccurate reporting. Gingrich claims to be speaking as an editor in disagreement with the other editors of the magazine, but this is not really accurate. Gingrich was not just the founder of the magazine but its guiding spirit, and a reappraisal from him is considerably more loaded than a simple difference of opinion among equals.

But there's more to the story. Erickson's draft was sent to Goodwin for approval. Then, in June, *Esquire* received a letter from James St. Clair, who turned out to be Goodwin's lawyer after all, demanding sixteen thousand dollars for Goodwin to pay the legal fees entailed in reaching the settlement. This came as a surprise to the management. Blinder was under the impression that the token payment of one thousand dollars was agreed upon; he also believed that this was to have been a transaction among gentlemen, not lawyers. *Esquire*'s house counsel, Ron Diana, replied to St. Clair on July 7. He said the magazine was completely unwilling to pay such a high fee, particularly because it continued to believe in the accuracy of Burlingham's article; Diana instead offered five thousand dollars. Arnold Hyatt, the shoe man, then resurfaced. He called Blinder to say that Goodwin was shocked at the belligerent tone of Diana's letter; Goodwin, all injured innocence, could not understand how things had gotten so unpleasant. Blinder was apparently persuaded by the call, and the $12,500 fee was arrived at. Blinder then sent Hyatt a case of champagne.

Out-of-court settlements are extremely complicated, or so I have found from talking to lawyers in the past couple of weeks. They're reached as a result of a combination of practical and ethical considerations. Generally speaking, though, if a magazine is willing to settle, the rule is this: if the magazine believes its article was right, it may settle for practical considerations and pay a token amount to avoid court costs. If the magazine is wrong, it may settle not only by paying off but also by printing a retraction, correction or apology. What is extremely rare—so rare that none of the lawyers I interviewed could recall a similar case—is for a magazine that believes it is right to pay off *and* print a retraction of sorts.

I can't quarrel with the financial settlement Goodwin got. I don't like it, but it's a business decision, I suppose. But Goodwin got the money *and* the apology. This is a tribute to him: he is as crafty and manipulative and brilliant as Bo Burlingham said he was. But it's a bad moment for this magazine. Abe Blinder told me that he had no problem with the settlement because: "There is no principle involved." I would like to state the principle involved. It's very simple. A magazine has an obligation to its writers and readers to stand by what it prints.

In any case, the Goodwin business is over. Bo Burlingham got $1,250 for his article and Dick Goodwin got $12,500 and an apology. There are all sorts of lessons to be drawn here, but the only one that seems to me at all worth mentioning is that I will henceforth try, when assigning articles on controversial subjects, to find writers who know the Tisch brothers.

In our conversation, Abe Blinder said that another reason he would probably not allow this column to run in *Esquire* was that Arnold Gingrich is dead and cannot defend himself. I am deeply sorry that Arnold is dead, for many reasons. For one thing, he was a man who could change his mind, and I like to think that by now he might have come around to Burlingham's way of seeing Dick Goodwin. For another, I think he meant it when he said what he did at the end of his monologue on Goodwin: "I've always said that this is a magazine of infinite surprises where people can say what they damn please, even to the extent of the editors disagreeing among themselves." If he were alive, I think that on those grounds he would have allowed me to print this column in the magazine: he would also have admitted that I outfoxed him just a little bit on that one small point.

One last thing. I speak only for myself, but I would like to apologize to Bo Burlingham.

*November, 1976*

# *Gourmet* Magazine

I'm not sure you can make a generalization on this basis, which is the basis of twice, but here goes: whenever I get married, I start buying *Gourmet* magazine. I think of it as my own personal bride's disease. The first time I started buying it was in 1967, when everyone my age in New York City spent hours talking about things like where to buy the best pistachio nuts. Someone recently told me that his marriage broke up during that period on account of veal Orloff, and I knew exactly what he meant. Hostesses were always making dinners that made you feel guilty, meals that took days to prepare and contained endless numbers of courses requiring endless numbers of plates resulting in an endless series of guests rising to help clear. Every time the conversation veered away from the food, the hostess looked hurt.

I got very involved in this stuff. Once I served a six-course Chinese dinner to twelve people, none of whom I still speak to, although not because of the dinner. I also specialized in little Greek appetizers that involved a great deal of playing with rice, and I once produced something known as the Brazilian national dish. Then, one night at a dinner party, a man I know looked up from his chocolate mousse and said, "Is this Julia's?" and I knew it was time to get off.

I can date that moment almost precisely—it was in December, 1972—because that's when I stopped buying *Gourmet* the first time around. And I can date that last *Gourmet* precisely because I have never thrown out a copy of the magazine. At the end of each month, I place it on the top of the kitchen bookshelf, and there it lies, undisturbed, forever. I have never once looked at a copy of *Gourmet* after its month was up. But I keep them because you never know when you might need to. One of the tricky things about the recipes in *Gourmet* is that they often refer back to recipes in previous copies of the magazine: for example, once a year, usually in January, *Gourmet* prints the recipe for pâte brisée, and if you throw out your January issue, you're sunk for the year. All the tart recipes thereafter call for "one recipe pâte brisée (January, 1976)" and that's that. The same thing holds for chicken stock. I realize that I have begun to sound as if I actually use the recipes in *Gourmet,* so I must stop here and correct that impression. I don't. I also realize that I have begun to sound as if I actually read *Gourmet,* and I'd better correct that impression too. I don't actually read it. I sort of look at it in a fairly ritualistic manner.

The first thing I turn to in *Gourmet* is the centerfold. The centerfold of the magazine contains the *Gourmet* menu of the month, followed by four color pages of pictures, followed by the recipes. In December the menu is usually for Christmas dinner, in November for Thanksgiving, in July for the Fourth, and in April—when I bought my first *Gourmet* in four years owing to my marriage that month to a man with a Cuisinart Food Processor—for Easter. The rest of the year there are fall luncheons and spring breakfasts, and so forth. But the point is not the menus but the pictures. The first picture each month is of the table of the month, and it is laid with the china and crystal and silver of the month. That most of the manufacturers of this china and crystal and silver advertise in *Gourmet* should not concern us now; that comes later in the ritual. The table and all the things on it look remarkably similar every issue: very formal, slightly stuffy, and extremely elegant in a cut-glass, old-moneyed way. The three pages of pictures that follow are of the food, which looks just as stuffy and formal and elegant as the table itself. It would never occur to anyone at *Gourmet* to take the kind of sleek, witty food photographs I associate with the *Life* "Great Dinners" series, or the crammed, decadent pictures the women's magazines specialize in. *Gourmet* gives you a full-page color picture of an incredibly serious rack of lamb persillé sitting on a somber Blue Canton platter by Mottahedeh Historic Charleston Reproductions sitting on a stiff eighteenth-century English mahogany table from Charles Deacon & Son—and it's no wonder I never cook anything from this magazine: the pictures are so reverent I almost feel I ought to pray to them.

After the centerfold I always turn to a section called "Sugar and Spice." This is the letters-to-the-editor department, and by all rights it should be called just plain "Sugar." I have never seen a letter in *Gourmet* that was remotely spicy, much less moderately critical. "I have culled so many fine recipes from your magazine that I feel it's time to do the sharing. . . ." "My husband and I have had many pleasant meals from recipes in *Gourmet* and we hope your readers will enjoy the following. . . ." Mrs. S. C. Rooney of Vancouver, B.C., writes to say that she and her husband leaf through *Gourmet* before every trip and would never have seen the Amalfi Drive but for the February, 1972, issue. "It is truly remarkable how you maintain such a high standard for every issue," she says. Almost every letter then goes on to present the writer's recipe—brownies Weinstein, piquant mushrooms Potthoff, golden marinade Wyeth, Parmesan puff Jupenlaz. "Sirs," writes Margy Newman of Beverly Hills, "recently I found myself with two ripe bananas, an upcoming weekend out of town, and an hour until dinnertime. With one eye on my food processor and the other on some prunes, I proceeded to invent Prune Banana Whip Newman." The recipe for one prune banana whip Newman (April, 1976) followed.

"You Asked For It" comes next. This is the section where readers write in for recipes from restaurants they have frequented and *Gourmet* provides them. I look at this section for two reasons: first, on the chance that someone has written in for the recipe for the tarte Tatin at Maxwell's Plum in New York, which I would like to know how to make, and second, for the puns. "Here is the scoop du jour," goes the introduction to peach ice cream Jordan Pond House. "We'd be berry happy," *Gourmet* writes in the course of delivering a recipe for blueberry blintzes. "Rather than waffling about, here is a recipe for chocolate waffles." "To satisfy your yen for tempura, here is Hibachi's shrimp tempura." I could go on, but I won't; I do want to mention, though, that the person who writes these also seems to write the headlines on the "Sugar and Spice" column—at least I think I detect the same fine hand in such headlines as "Curry Favor," "The Berry Best" and "Something Fishy."

I skip the travel pieces, many of which are written by ladies with three names. "If Provence did not exist, the poets would be forced to invent it, for it is a lyrical landscape and to know it is to be its loving captive for life." Like that. Then I skip the restaurant reviews. *Gourmet* never prints unfavorable restaurant reviews; in fact, one of its critics is so determined not to find fault anywhere that he recently blamed himself for a bad dish he was served at the Soho Charcuterie: "The potatoes that came with it (savoyarde?—hard to tell) were disappointingly nondescript and cold, but I seemed to be having bad luck with potatoes *wherever* I went." Then I skip the special features on eggplant and dill and the like, because I have to get on to the ads.

*Gourmet* carries advertisements for a wide array of upper-class consumer goods (Rolls-Royce, De Beers diamonds, Galliano, etc.); the thing is to compare these ads to the editorial content of the magazine. I start by checking out the *Gourmet* holiday of the month—in May, 1976, for example, it was Helsinki—and then I count the number of ads in the magazine for things Finnish. Then I like to check the restaurants reviewed in the front against the restaurant ads in the back. Then, of course, I compare the china, silver and crystal in the menu of the month against the china, silver and crystal ads. All this is quite satisfying and turns out about the way you might suspect.

After that, I am pretty much through looking at *Gourmet* magazine. And where has it gotten me, you may ask. I've been trying to figure that out myself. Last April, when I began my second round, I think I expected that this time I would get around to cooking something from it. Then May passed and I failed to make the rhubarb tart pictured in the centerfold and I gave up in the recipe department. At that point, it occurred to me that perhaps I bought *Gourmet* because I figured it was the closest I would ever get to being a gentile. But that's not it either. The real reason, I'm afraid, has simply to do with food and life, particularly married life. "Does everyone who gets married talk about furniture?" my friend Bud Trillin once asked. No. Only for a while. After that you talk about pistachio nuts.

*December, 1976*

# The *Detroit News*

A few months ago, Seth Kantor went and laid an egg. Kantor works in Washington as an investigative reporter for the *Detroit News,* and in October, 1976, he broke a big one, a scoop on the Michigan Senate race, a front-page story that he clearly thinks ought to have earned him praise, if not prize nominations; instead, it got him nothing but criticism. Two columnists on his own paper attacked him. Mike Royko of the *Chicago Daily News* suggested that the *Detroit News* be awarded a large bronze laundry hamper for "the most initiative in poking around in somebody else's dirty underwear." Even Kantor's wife thought he went a little overboard.

Kantor's story said that Democrat Don Riegle, a Michigan congressman then running for the Senate, had had an affair in 1969 with a young woman who tape-recorded several of their conversations with his permission. (In 1969 Riegle was married to his first wife; he is now married to his second.) The *News* printed selected portions of the taped transcripts. Seth Kantor claims that the episode "tells you a lot about a man's judgment as well as his stability." A *News* editorial that endorsed Riegle's opponent Marvin Esch claimed that the story revealed Riegle's "arrogance, immaturity, cold-bloodedness and consuming political ambition."

The voters of Michigan apparently felt otherwise. The day Kantor's story appeared, Riegle had slipped to a bare 1 percent edge in the polls; on election day three weeks later he won the Senate seat by a 6 percent margin, and his staff considered sending the *News* a telegram reading: "Thanks. We couldn't have done it without you."

In the year or so since Fanne Foxe jumped into the Tidal Basin, journalists have begun to debate a number of extremely perplexing questions concerning the private lives of political figures. How much does the public have the right to know? How much does an editor have the right to determine what the public has a right to know? Where do you cross the line into invasion of privacy? Last summer, in the most successful book promotion stunt ever pulled off, Elizabeth Ray brought down Wayne Hays—but she was an editor's dream, the-mistress-on-the-payroll-who-can't-type. What about mistresses who *can* type? Editors justify printing just about anything about a politician on the grounds of character. Are those adequate grounds? These questions are worth thinking about, but they all assume that decisions on what to print will be made by responsible journalists. As it happens, that may not be the correct assumption in the case of the *Detroit News.*

The *News* is the largest afternoon newspaper in America (circulation 613,000), and until last year, when the *Detroit Free Press* overtook it, it was one of the few big-city afternoon papers that sold more copies than the local morning paper. The decline in *News* circulation is generally attributed to a number of factors: editorial lethargy, a rising number of white-collar workers within the city as well as overall population decline, and an increased antagonism toward the paper in Detroit's black community. On the editorial page, the *News* supports civil rights; but following the 1967 riots, publisher Peter Clark bricked up the first-floor windows of the *News* building; the paper also began printing a daily roundup of minor crimes, identifying suspects by race. In 1971, under a photograph, the *News* ran this caption: "Milton B. Allen, fifty-three, of Baltimore, isn't letting the fact that he's the city's first Negro state's attorney deter him from his crusade against narcotics, crime and corruption." Last year, Mike McCormick, news editor of the *News,* sent his staff a memo that leaked to Mayor Coleman Young, who attacked it in a widely reported speech. "We are aiming our product," McCormick wrote, "at the people who make more than $18,000 a year and are in the twenty-eight to forty group. Keep a lookout for and then play—well—the stories city desk develops and aims at this group. They should be obvious: they won't have a damn thing to do with Detroit and its internal problems."

Since 1959, the *News* has been run by Martin S. Hayden, a conservative who was one of the few editors of a major newspaper to oppose the printing of the Pentagon Papers. Hayden is the last of a breed—a power broker as well as an editor; one *News* political reporter recalls a recent Detroit mayoral campaign in which Hayden persuaded *both* candidates to run. In 1969, Hayden and publisher Clark were supporters of the missile program; during the ABM debate in Congress, Hayden sent a memo to the *News* Washington bureau that read: "The Washington staff should watch our editorial page, know our policy and help support it" by looking for "interpretative pieces and sidebars that help drive home the editorial point of view." Hayden insists he never asks reporters to slant the news, but several journalists who have been offered jobs in the Washington bureau got the impression that he expected them to investigate Democrats slightly more carefully than Republicans.

Now sixty-four, Hayden is retiring in June, and in the last year his power has become less than absolute. In 1975, a group of *News* employees met to discuss ways to improve the paper; they discovered that part of the problem was that the paper was perceived as stodgy and conservative. This group, which subsequently became known as the Kiddie Committee, set to work to hire younger reporters and columnists who were "with it" or "hip" or merely bearded. Meanwhile, publisher Clark offered a column to the *News*'s most outspoken critic, a local talk-show host named Lou Gordon. Gordon and the new columnists began to snipe regularly at each other and at the way the *News* handled various stories. Hayden was not amused. "It's too much of a discussion of the newspaper business," he says. "I've always disliked reporters who make themselves part of the story. It wasn't the way I was brought up." Hayden continues to keep a close eye on the Washington bureau, while the other editors deal directly with the local staff; as a result, the paper occasionally seems schizophrenic. During the Riegle-Esch campaign, for instance, two young local political reporters wrote a story saying that Republican Esch had lied about his role in passing a piece of legislation; twelve days later, John Peterson of the Washington bureau wrote a story saying that Esch's lie was only a *little* lie.

Seth Kantor reported directly to Martin Hayden on all three stories he wrote about Don Riegle. The first, which ran in September, said that Riegle had signed his estranged wife's name to a tax rebate check in 1971 and then failed to give her half the refund. This was followed by a story quoting a Jack Anderson study that called Riegle one of the ten most unpopular members of Congress. Both stories were attacked by Riegle: the first was clearly a shabby episode in an acrimonious divorce, the second a harsh way of describing an unsurprising fact—congressmen who switch parties (as Riegle did, in 1973) are bound to be unpopular. Then Kantor got the tapes story.

In 1976, following the Elizabeth Ray revelations, a writer named Robin Moore (*The Green Berets, The Happy Hooker*) came to Washington to write a paperback about congressional sex. He was introduced to one Bette Jane Ackerman, who had had an affair with Riegle in 1969 while she was an unpaid staff worker in his office; during that period, she made some tapes of her conversations with him and supposedly replayed them like love letters while she was home sick. Eventually, the romance ended, Riegle divorced his wife and married another staff member. Last summer, Miss Ackerman accepted five hundred dollars from Robin

Moore for her help as a go-between with other Washington women, and she played her tapes for *New York News* reporter Joe Volz, who was then working with Moore. The tapes are predictably adolescent, childishly dirty and thoroughly egomaniacal. "I'll always love you," Riegle tells Miss Ackerman. "I—I—God, I feel such super love for you. By the way, the newsletter should start arriving."

Kantor got hold of a transcript of the tapes. He also obtained some love letters Riegle wrote to Miss Ackerman. And at some point, with editor Hayden's approval, he drew up and signed an agreement with Miss Ackerman's lawyer, David Taylor, pledging that he would not use her name in the stories. Kantor then flew to Detroit and went to confront Riegle with the story. Kantor's version will give you an idea of the tenor of the meeting:

"He agreed to meet me with a lawyer. They had a tape recorder. I had a tape recorder. I asked him about this relationship with this unpaid staff worker, taped with his knowledge, and I got a strong blast at both the *Detroit News* and at me. He said it was a well-known fact in Washington that I had been assigned by my editor to get him. I asked him who had told him that. He refused to tell me. He said I was absolutely the worst journalist in Washington. I said, Well, if I can't be the best, I'd just as soon be the worst. Well, he said, we all have to make a living."

Both Seth Kantor and Martin Hayden deny that anyone at the *News* was out to get Don Riegle—but somebody must have been; there's no other way to explain the decision to run the story Kantor turned in. Written in pulp-magazine style, it's loaded with phrases like "sex-tainted," "provocative brunet," "kiss-and-playback romance," "telltale tapes," "boudoir antics," and so forth. It refers to Miss Ackerman as "Dorothy" —allegedly her code name on the tapes—and fails to mention the fact that she was paid by Robin Moore. It also leaves out something that Kantor and Hayden knew—that Miss Ackerman had been what newspaper reporters call "close" with South Korean lobbyist Tongsun Park, as well as several other congressmen. The lead of the story says that Riegle once described the affair as "more important than 'a lousy subcommittee hearing.'" Later in the article, it becomes clear that Riegle used the expression in a casual, offhand way: "In one of their conversations, Riegle said he had to break away 'to go to a lousy subcommittee hearing now.'" Kantor added sanctimoniously: "It is in the subcommittees that Congress does its basic legislative work."

The article backfired totally, of course. *News* columnists Lou Gordon and Fred Girard wrote columns protesting it. The Associated Press and United Press International refused to run the story the day it broke. Says AP executive editor Louis Boccardi: "We try to make a decision like this based on whether there's some relevance to the individual's public responsibility, and we couldn't satisfy ourselves that was the case here." Within days, Riegle was the recipient of a wave of sympathy; he took the offensive, attacking the *News* and charging the paper with conspiring with his opponent to smear him.

Two weeks later, Saul Friedman of the *Detroit Free Press* wrote the other half of the story—he identified Miss Ackerman by name, linked her to Park, and revealed the financial details of her transaction with Moore. Which proved that in a healthy, competitive, two-newspaper town, the public is occasionally subjected to twice as much trash.

When I interviewed Martin Hayden in Detroit after the election, he did not believe he had made a mistake in running the Riegle story. "Seth said that all this information was coming out in Moore's book," said Hayden. "What if the book came out and people said, 'Did you know about this?'" Did Hayden ever consider not printing the transcript of the tapes? "Not after we had them. Without the tapes I don't know if there would have been any story. The question was of his judgment, not his sexual morality." Did he think the story was heavy-handed? "As a matter of fact, we went easy. Before we were through we became convinced this was not an isolated case." Did Hayden meet with Kantor or any *News* editors to discuss whether the story should be printed? "No. I handled it. Whatever blame there is is mine."

Should Hayden have printed the story? Probably not—the fact that it would eventually be printed in a quickie paperback is hardly justification. But if he decided to go ahead, he ought to have printed the whole story—including Miss Ackerman's name and details about her financial transactions concerning the tapes. In order to nail Riegle, the *News* gave up half the story.

Was the piece justified on the grounds that, finally, Riegle's character was revealed? No. Anyone who reads Riegle's book, *O Congress,* is perfectly able to perceive his "arrogance, immaturity, cold-bloodedness and consuming political ambition." Among other things.

Should Hayden have used the tapes? No. I can't make a rule about what constitutes an invasion of privacy, but I know one when I see one.

For some time after I came back from Detroit, I wondered what all this proved. Certainly it was clear that the voters of Michigan were more sophisticated than Seth Kantor and Martin S. Hayden, but that wasn't much of a point: so is my cat. Then, on November 7, Larry Flynt published a full-page advertisement in the *Washington Post* promising to pay $25,000 to any woman who would tell her story about sex with a congressman to *Hustler* magazine, and I looked for some way to tie that in, but I couldn't. I'm afraid, in fact, that I can't come up with a real point to any of this. Which may be the point. Nobody really cares. Newspaper editors have stumbled into a whole new area they're now allowed to publish stories about, and they're publishing ridiculous, irrelevant, hypocritical, ugly little articles that aren't dirty enough for *Hustler* or relevant enough for the papers that print them. "Maybe I'm on the wrong side of the pendulum swinging," Seth Kantor said to me. Maybe so.

*February, 1977*

# The *Ontario Bulletin*

Two years ago, my husband bought a cooperative in the Ontario Apartments in Washington, D.C. The Ontario is an old building as Washington apartment buildings go, turn of the century, to be imprecise, and it has high ceilings, considerable woodwork, occasional marble and views of various capital sights. It also has the *Ontario Bulletin*. The *Ontario Bulletin* is a mimeographed newsletter that arrives every month or so in the mailbox. It is supplemented by numerous urgent memos and elevator notices; many of these concern crime. The Ontario is located in what is charitably called a marginal neighborhood, and all of us who live there look for signs that it is on the verge of becoming less marginal. The fact that the local movie theater is switching from Spanish-language films to English-language films is considered a good sign. The current memo in the elevator is now: "During the past eight weeks, FIVE ONTARIO WOMEN HAVE HAD THEIR PURSES SNATCHED on the grounds or close by. Three of these events occurred this week." This memo, written by Sue Lindgren, chairperson, Security Committee, goes on to state: "Fortunately, none of the victims was seriously injured and no building keys were lost." We were all relieved to read this, though I suspect that Christine Turpin was primarily relieved to read the part about the keys. Mrs. Turpin was president of the Ontario during the crime wave of May, 1976, when she wrote a particularly fine example of what I think of as the Turpin School of memo writing:

"There have been *three purse snatchings* at the Ontario's front door in the last *two weeks* causing *lock changes twice* in the same period. All three incidents occurred in daylight hours; the three 'victims'—all women—were returning from grocery stores on Columbia Road. Two of the three had ignored repeated and publicized advice: DO NOT CARRY BUILDING KEYS IN YOUR POCKETBOOKS. They also ignored other personal safety precautions. Much as we sympathize with them over their frightening experience and over the loss of their personal belongings, the fact remains that had these 'victims' heeded the warnings, everyone at the Ontario would have been spared the inconvenience of a second lock/key change in two weeks as well as the expenditure of $250 for replacements."

As far as I can tell, several of the early warnings Mrs. Turpin refers to appeared in the *Ontario Bulletin,* but I can hardly blame the "victims" for not noticing them. Until recently, the *Ontario Bulletin* was written by Mildred A. Pappas, who appears to be as blithe and good-humored as Mrs. Turpin is the opposite. Here and there Mrs. Pappas tucks in a late-breaking crime story: "As we were going to press Security Chairman Sue Lindgren called to say that the cigarette machine in the basement had been vandalized and that both cigarettes and some change were missing. There were no known suspects at the time of the call." But Mrs. Pappas has a firm editorial philosophy which she expressed in the January, 1975, *Bulletin:* "Both the trivial and the important are vital in portraying a clear picture of life in the Ontario—or anywhere else." And she has such a charming way with the trivial that her readers really ought to be forgiven their apparent tendency to skip over the important. In the February, 1975, *Bulletin,* for example, Mrs. Pappas does mention the business of not putting keys into pocketbooks, but that item pales next to the report on the revival of a limp African violet at the Houseplant Clinic, and it fades into insignificance next to the tantalizing mention of the removal of a hornets' nest from Elsie Carpenter's dining room window.

The information on the hornets' nest appeared in

a regular feature of the *Bulletin* called "News and Notes," which includes birthdays, operations, recent houseguests and distinguished achievements of residents, as well as small bits of miscellaneous information like the announcement of the founding of the Ad Hoc Friends of the Pool Table Committee. Other regular sections of the publication are "The Travelers Return," a list of recent trips by residents; and "Committee Reports," summaries of the doings of the various building committees, of which there are nine. (This figure does not include the committee for the pool table, which has since disbanded, having successfully restored the table to use in the basement Green Room, which was recently and unaccountably painted yellow during the 1976 Painting Project.) The Ontario is surrounded by trees and gardens, so the *Bulletin* often mentions the planting of a new azalea or juniper tree, and it recently devoted an entire page to the final chapter of the eight-year controversy of the Great Red Oak, cut down on August 27, 1976, after the board of directors overruled what was known as the "wait and see" policy of the High Tree Subcommittee. Articles like these are often illustrated with simple drawings of birds and leaves. Occasionally, a photograph is used, but only on a major story like the flap over the water bill.

Ontario residents first learned of the water-bill flap in a July, 1975, *Bulletin* article headlined A SHOCKING BILL FOR A SHOCKING WASTE: "Chairman Chris Turpin has just announced that a staggering (and unbudgeted) $1,660.94 water bill for the last quarter has just been received, adding that the amount is more than *three* times the amount for the preceding quarter. A wrong billing? No. Uncommon usage for bad water, etc.? No. . . . The water company has advanced the opinion that only one malfunctioning toilet allowed to run continuously can be the cause. . . . The chairman stated that the board will decide on a method of payment of the unprecedented bill at its July meeting, the alternatives being (1) to find the resident or residents responsible and to bill accordingly, or (2) to specially assess *all* residents (owners and tenants alike) approximately $10 each to settle the bill."

For a month, we anxiously awaited word of what was up. Would ten dollars be added to the maintenance? Or would Chairman Turpin lead the Ad Hoc Committee on the Unprecedented Water Bill through each apartment in search of the hypothetical malfunctioning toilet? Finally, the July *Bulletin* appeared, with a terse report suggesting that the investigation was closing in: the prime suspect turned out to be not some irresponsible resident but the building's thirty-five-year-old water meter, which had just been removed for inspection by the water company. Meanwhile, Clarence K. Streit, a resident who was apparently unaware that human error was about to be ruled out, made a guest appearance in the *Bulletin* as the author of the Flask Water Dollar Saver. "It is quite practical," he wrote, "to save three pints of water every time one flushes a toilet. We have been doing it for a couple of years." According to Streit, if everyone in the building placed three pint flasks in his toilet tank, then Ontario could save 150,000 gallons of water a year—or, as he put it, *150,000* gallons of water a year. Mrs. Pappas urged residents who took up Streit's suggestion to submit their names for publication in order to encourage others. No one did; at least I assume no one did from the fact that Mrs. Pappas never again referred to the Flask Water Dollar Saver Plan. In the August *Bulletin,* however, the water meter was definitely fingered; it turned out to be not just out of order but thoroughly obsolete. A photograph of the new water meter appeared as an illustration.

If I have any complaint at all about the *Ontario Bulletin,* it is simply that its even-handed approach occasionally leaves something to be desired. Accurate reporting was simply not enough to convey the passions engendered by the paint selections of the 1976 Painting Project, nor was it adequate to describe the diabolical maneuverings of President Turpin and the

Ontario board in the face of these passions. Residents who read the loving tribute in the August *Bulletin* to the Great Red Oak and the account of its mysterious incurable disease could hardly have been prepared for the stunning moment at the annual meeting in September when it was moved that no tree be cut down without a membership vote. Mrs. Pappas's low-key description of the restored iron grille entrance doors— "Unfortunately, the 'Ontario' inscription now faces the interior of the building since it could not be relocated from its solid iron casting to the outside"—does not quite do justice to the situation.

And I cannot imagine that *Bulletin* readers were in any position to judge the item in March, 1976, which announced Dr. Allan Angerio's resignation as House Maintenance Committee Chairman. "In protest of the Board's sanction of extensive remodeling in a neighboring apartment, Dr. Allan Angerio has resigned five months after his appointment. In a recently circulated letter to all residents Dr. Angerio states that during the extended period of renovation he was 'unable to use my apartment for either business or pleasure.' He also states that his letter has engendered a considerable response from the membership, many of whom have indicated interest in a proposed revision of the Bylaws and House Rules of the Corporation to preclude further extensive structural 'modernization' efforts in the Ontario." This is certainly a fair summary of what happened—but it is not enough. I know. I am married to the man who hired the contractor who accidentally drilled the hole into Dr. Angerio's bedroom wall.

In any case, mine are small complaints. The main function of a newspaper is to let its readers know what's going on; I doubt that there are many communities that are served as well by their local newspapers as this tiny community is by the *Ontario Bulletin*. And I would feel even more warmly toward the publication than I do but for the fear I have, each month, that I will pick it up to read: "The residents of 605 had a fight last Thursday night over the fact that one person in the apartment never closes her closet doors." I like neighborhoods, you see, but I worry about neighbors. Fortunately, my husband and I also have an apartment in New York. And I was extremely pleased several weeks ago when we moved to new quarters there in an extremely unfriendly-looking brownstone on an extremely haughty block. In the course of the week's move, we carried some garbage out of the apartment and left it on the street for the garbage collectors. Ten minutes later—*ten minutes later*—a memo arrived from the 74th Street Block Association concerning the block rules on refuse. I'm not going to quote from it. All I want to say is that its author, Emma Preziosi, while not in the same league with Christine Turpin, definitely shows promise.

*March, 1977*

# The Revitalization
of Clay Filter:
Yet Another Passage

On the surface, Clay Filter would appear to have had everything he had ever wanted. (His name is fictitious.) The ginger-haired magazine editor might not have wanted the middle-age spread that occasionally caused his shirt buttons to pop off, but otherwise he had achieved his life's dream. He had *gained his authenticity.* He had spent most of his Deadline Decade dreaming of running his own magazine, and finally he had come to do so. He lived in a beautiful apartment with a double-height living room which, had it faced south, which it did not, would have reflected the city he had built a magazine to. He had spent ten years off and on with the same woman, in a relationship I would call an *Off-and-On Relationship;* he had served as her Mentor (see pp. 14, 27, 51–2, 54, 76–7, 85, 109, 128, 131–2, 189–90, 280, 293; see also Career Women and Mentors, pp. 128, 132–5, 225, 226, 227), and he had only two complaints about her: he worried she would write about him someday and disguise him as thinly as she disguised everyone else she wrote about; and he occasionally became irritated at her uncanny ability to predict every adult crisis that was to befall him and then say, "I told you so," as soon as it did. Sometimes she went even further by insisting he had had a crisis when he thought he had merely had a bad cabdriver, but when he accused her of a priori reasoning, she simply reminded him that he was a classic wunderkind (see pp. 189–98) and that all wunderkinder tend to deny they have mid-life crises. He dozed off as she rattled on about patterns of wunderkinder: "They were afraid to admit they were not all-knowing. Afraid to let anyone come too close. Afraid to stop filling their time with external challenges they could probably surmount, for fear of glimpsing that vast and treacherous interior which seems insurmountable. Afraid that the moment they let down their guard, someone might ridicule them, expose them, move in on their weaknesses and reduce them again to the powerlessness of a little boy. It is not their wives they are afraid of. It is themselves. That part of themselves I have called the Inner Custodian, which is derivative of parents and other figures from childhood." She paused. "Do you understand what I'm saying, darling?"

Clay Filter snapped awake and nodded comprehendingly. The truth, though, was that he could never figure out what she was talking about when she went on in this way. He knew it sold magazines, and books, and that someone must understand it, but he knew he didn't, and he wasn't sure what he could do about it if he did. He had pushed himself through the Trying Twenties and the Catch Thirties and the Switch Forties. He had fought the fight between his Merger Self and his Seeker Self, giving in to his Merger Self on only two or three occasions, if you counted living arrangements. He had survived the Seesaw Years and the Pulling Up Roots Years, and now here he was, and part of the problem was that he wasn't sure just where he was at. Years before, he had altered his birth date in *Who's Who*, and he now no longer knew for certain how old he was. Freud would call this *self-deception*, and Jung would call this *silliness*, and Erikson would call this *ridiculous vanity*, but I call it *The Refusal to Deal with the Age-Forty Crucible*. The catch was that he no longer knew whether he was at the tail end of the Switch Forties or on the verge of the Fractious Fifties, and while he didn't much care one way or the other about it, the woman he had been with for ten years in the *Off-and-On Relationship* cared deeply.

"The crisis will emerge . . . around fifty," she said. "And although its wallop will be greater, the jolt may be just what is needed to prod the resigned middle-ager toward seeking revitalization."

"I'm sick of all this talk about my crisis!" Clay Filter shouted. "I'm too old to have a crisis!"

"It's never too late to have a crisis," she said. "Anyway, darling, don't think of it as a crisis. Think of it as a *passage*. Does that help?"

"No, it doesn't help!" he shouted. "Crisis is a perfectly good word. Why coin another?"

At moments like this, she wondered whether he might not turn out to be an exception to all her theories. He had an explosive temper. Perhaps he would spend his crisis in little bursts, piggyback one mini-crisis atop another and avoid the big bang. Just the other night, unaccountably, he had blown up at her for using piggyback as a verb. Then, when she defended herself, he threatened to rip the italic bar from her typewriter. Outbursts like that were becoming more frequent. She realized it was more important than ever for her to be supportive in order to help him find his way up the developmental ladder.

"Each one of us has our own *step-style*," she said one day as he stared, preoccupied, at the rug, "the characteristic manner in which we attack the tasks of development and react to the efforts we make. Some of us take a series of cautious steps forward, then one or two back, then a long skip up to a higher level. There are those of us who thrive on setting up sink-or-swim situations. . . . Others, when face to face with each task, side step it for a time in a flurry of extraneous activity."

"Do you think I should buy *The Village Voice*?" he asked, looking up.

"This could be your long skip up to a higher level," she replied.

"I don't know anything about money," he said.

"On the other hand," she said, "this could be your flurry of extraneous activity."

"This isn't my flurry of extraneous activity," he said. "That comes later, when I recklessly fly off to the Bahamas."

"Then perhaps it's your sink-or-swim activity."

"I think I'll let Felix make the deal," said Clay Filter.

She made a note for a new syndrome. She would call it *You Can Turn Over the Closing to the Broker, But YOU Pay the Mortgage*. She would tell him about it at some point, but now he had fallen asleep.

Some months later, when he awoke, he discovered that Felix had got things backward. In the course of buying *The Village Voice* for Clay Filter's magazine, Felix had accidentally sold Filter's magazine to *The Village Voice*. This was an extremely confusing turn of events. Confusing turns of events often precipitate crises. Just as often, they do not. It is possible that had Clay Filter realized either of these points, he might have been able to avert what was to happen. Instead, he started a new magazine and began flying back and forth across the country each week. He was spreading himself too thin, except for the aforementioned part of him that was simply spreading itself. One morning, after he stepped off the Red Eye from Los Angeles, he was forced to stand for two hours in the freezing cold at Kennedy airport, and when he finally got a taxi, the driver was surly and unpleasant and a reader of *Cue*. This so infuriated Filter that he marched into a board of directors meeting and demanded a raise, two houses and a limousine. The board of directors, already upset about the profit picture, turned Filter down in an extremely acrimonious session and then went off to plot ways to sell their stock.

"I think I'm having a crisis," he said to her that night.

"Don't be silly, darling," she replied. "You merely had a bad cabdriver."

When the crisis finally began, he recklessly flew off to the Bahamas. When he returned, he lost his temper and alienated the principal stockholder, who decided to sell out to an Australian. In the end, Clay Filter got one and a half million dollars and the love and devotion of several dozen employees who had previously been ambivalent toward him. But he lost his magazine, and his magazine was his life. He had offers, and he had ideas, and he would return, but there was a nagging part of himself—the part of himself physiologists call the *Brain*—that suspected that all of this could have been avoided. He suggested this to her.

"Wrong, darling, wrong," she said. "All of it was necessary. And more than that, it was thrilling. It was so *predictable*. The wallop. The jolt. Just what is needed to prod the resigned middle-ager toward seeking revitalization." She smiled. "Oh, darling," she said. "I'm so happy for you."

*April, 1977*

# Double-Crostics

It is one of the great surprises of my adult life that I am not particularly good at doing the Double-Crostic. When I was growing up, I thought that being able to do the Double-Crostic was an adult attribute, not unlike buying hard-cover books, and that eventually I would grow into it. My mother, who was indirectly responsible for this misapprehension, was a whiz at Double-Crostics and taught me how to do them. In those days, the Double-Crostic was available through three sources: every week in the *Saturday Review,* every other week in the *New York Times Magazine* and twice a year in a Simon and Schuster anthology containing fifty or so new puzzles. The first two puzzles in each anthology were geared to beginners—to idiots, to be more precise—and I could usually solve one of them in about a month, using an atlas, a dictionary, a thesaurus, a Bartlett's and an occasional tip from my mother, who would never have been caught dead using any source material at all. There are many things I will never forgive my mother for, but heading the list is the fact that she did the Double-Crostic in ink.

Back then, the Double-Crostic was called the Kingsley Double-Crostic after Elizabeth S. Kingsley, who invented the form and eventually passed the puzzle-making on to Doris Nash Wortman. I had a very clear idea of what Mesdames Kingsley and Wortman looked like: jolly fat gray-haired ladies with large bosoms and cameo brooches and voluminous silk dresses covered with little flowers. As it turns out, I was right. Mrs. Wortman was succeeded in 1967 by one Thomas H. Middleton, and until I began researching this column, I had always imagined that he was Mrs. Wortman's loyal disciple, a faithful fan who had spent years corresponding with her and sending in his own constructions to be printed in the fans section in Double-Crostic anthologies. Presumably he had been rewarded upon her death with the puzzles. As it turns out, I was wrong. He got the job by being Norman Cousins's brother-in-law.

I called up Thomas Middleton the other day to find out about his life. He told me that he lives in Brentwood, in Los Angeles, that he is an actor and can currently be seen in a Life Savers commercial, and that George C. Scott loves Double-Crostics. He said he constructs one hundred seventy-five puzzles a year himself and in addition writes a column on language for the *Saturday Review* in which he has twice tackled the subject of "hopefully." "My feeling is that 'hopefully' is here to stay," he said. In short, it wasn't much of a phone call, and I came away from it with the impression that Middleton regards the making of Double-Crostics as a job, not a passion. This made perfect sense—ever since he took them over, I have regarded the *solving* of Double-Crostics as a job, not a passion— but it hardly seemed fair. In any case, I got quite sentimental about Elizabeth Kingsley and Doris Nash Wortman, about whom I knew next to nothing, and set about learning a bit.

Elizabeth Seelman Kingsley was born in Brooklyn in about 1878 and grew up working scrambled-word puzzles in *St. Nicholas* magazine; after graduating from Wellesley in 1898, she became an English teacher until her marriage. During the national crossword-puzzle binge of the 1920s, she worked several crosswords and then remarked: "How futile! There is a certain fun in the thrill of the puzzle, to be sure, but what is the goal?" A few years later, at a Wellesley reunion, she became so disturbed at the undergraduates' enthusiasm for James Joyce and Gertrude Stein that she determined to do something about it. "Suddenly it dawned upon me," she said years later, "that a puzzle which stimulated the imagination and heightened an appreciation of fine literature by reviewing English and American poetry and prose masters would be a puzzle *with* a goal." Thus was born the first Double-Crostic, and in 1934 Mrs. Kingsley sold her first puzzle—and the rights to the name—to the *Saturday Review of Literature*.

It is not easy to describe a Double-Crostic, but basically it consists of a series of definitions to which one supplies answers. The letters of the answers are transferred into a diagram that eventually spells out a quotation from a work of literature. The initials of the correct answers spell out the author's name and the work from which the quote is taken, and if you have managed to follow this so far, you will no doubt have figured out that Mrs. Kingsley's puzzles relied heavily on the works of Shakespeare, Keats, Defoe and the like and utterly shunned Joyce, Stein and any other writer she thought of as less than a master.

Mrs. Kingsley, who was widowed, lived for many years in the Henry Hudson Hotel in Manhattan, where she worked out her puzzles using anagram blocks on a piece of felt. She earned about ten thousand dollars a year—not a great deal, even for a small-scale literary heroine, which in a way she was. She was often referred to as Queen Elizabeth, and various Double-Crostic fans fussed over her; Arthur Hays Sulzberger invited her to lunch at the *New York Times,* and Philip Hamburger profiled her in *The New Yorker*.

She told Hamburger that *h*'s were the bane of her existence, with *f*'s and *w*'s close behind; these letters were constantly left over and she was constantly forced to do something with them. "Powwow" was a favorite answer; "tow-row" set off a terrible fracas among her fans. Once, a reader wrote in to accuse her of an overwhelming affection for Vedic divinities. "Vedic divinities are not a spontaneous choice for definitions," Mrs. Kingsley replied. "They are a godsend after hours of juggling. If you were constructing a puzzle and had letters left over and they made a Vedic divinity, what would *you* do?" Mrs. Kingsley carried a notebook with her and was constantly jotting down words that might someday come in handy. She told Philip Hamburger: "Here's 'wow-wow.' A lovely thing! *Four w's.* 'Hiwi hiwi.' What a word! Means a small marine fish in New Zealand. And 'chiffchaff'—just an English bird. All my people need do is look up 'chiffchaff' under 'willow wren.' Ah, yes! 'Dingdong.' *And* 'omoo,' a romance in the South Seas. Don't tell *me* people aren't better educated for knowing these things!"

In her later years, Mrs. Kingsley became a small-scale prima donna. According to Margaret Farrar, the grand old lady of the *New York Times* crossword puzzle, she talked of nothing but Double-Crostics. She dropped the names of her famous fans, who included Elmer Rice, Ogden Nash and Frank Sullivan. Helen Barrow, who designed the puzzle books for Simon and Schuster, saved several of Mrs. Kingsley's letters; in them she complains about her harried life: she was constructing some two hundred puzzles a year, and it wasn't getting any easier. Finally, in 1952, Queen Elizabeth retired—she died in 1957—and she was succeeded by Princess Doris.

Doris Nash Wortman, born in New Jersey in 1890, was a Smith graduate and past president of the National Puzzlers' League. She worshiped Mrs. Kingsley; she had been proofreading Double-Crostics for her since 1939, when she had submitted an extremely complicated construction—a valentine to her husband, Elbert—to a fans section. On the evidence, she appears to have been among the most good-natured women who ever lived. Her puzzles had a light-hearted quality Mrs. Kingsley would never have tolerated; she introduced modern writers and witty quotations and definitions. Her fans sections contained lovely tidbits about each of her correspondents; she was a gracious, chattering den mother to her troop. Her letters and book introductions are positively ebullient. "WOW! What an ad!!" she wrote Helen Barrow when the fiftieth Double-Crostic anthology was published. "Everyone thinks Series 50 *utter,* especially I!"

Mrs. Wortman lived in Jackson Heights, Queens, with Elbert, a sometime advertising man, and according to her daughter, DeNyse Pinkerton, she worked all the time. "She started at five a.m. and worked until eleven p.m." said Mrs. Pinkerton. "It was ghastly. The worst part was my father. He had had one glorious failure after another. She really paid the rent, and he made her make him a three-course dinner every night." Mrs. Wortman earned about fifteen thousand dollars a year.

Doris Nash Wortman had only two problems. One was Elbert. The other was that she occasionally irritated her puzzlers by using made-up expressions in order to use up left-over letters. Once, for example, she printed a definition reading, "The corn is evidently higher than Hammerstein thought." The answer was "giraffe's eye." Also, Mrs. Wortman had an unfortunate tendency to let her politics seep into her puzzles. Laura Z. Hobson, the novelist and author of *Gentleman's Agreement,* was a Double-Crostic solver; one day, while having lunch with *Saturday Review* editor Norman Cousins, she brought up the subject of Mrs. Wortman's leanings.

As Mrs. Hobson recalls it: "I said, 'Say, Cuzz, doesn't anybody edit those things?' 'Why, L.H., what's wrong?' he said. I told him that that very week there was a clue that said, 'Describing some of the people in the South,' and the answer was 'blacks and tans.' He blanched. For the *Saturday Review* to talk about blacks and tans! I gave him other examples. One thing she frequently did was to have the definition indicate a noun though the answer was a participle. Once, for instance, she had used 'A gift for an institution,' and the answer was 'endowing' instead of 'endowment.' It was just sloppy. Cuzz was appalled and asked me to edit the puzzles, and I have done it ever since. Twice I asked her to kill puzzles completely. One of the quotes was anti-labor, and the other was a John Masefield poem on the death of President Kennedy. I don't think that's what you expect to come across in a puzzle. In my opinion she was nowhere near as good as Mrs. Kingsley."

After Mrs. Wortman's death, Elbert decided to carry on the puzzles—something even his wife had thought he was not equipped to do. He began lurking in the offices of the *Saturday Review* with sample puzzles. He claimed he had done all his wife's work. He threatened to sue. "It was somewhat sticky," says Norman Cousins. A few fans had submitted tryout puzzles; in addition, Cousins contacted his sister's husband and asked him to take a crack at it. Laura Hobson judged the entries, voted for Middleton, and that was that.

Mrs. Hobson thinks Tom Middleton does a bang-up job, and so does Margaret Farrar. I think he prints too many definitions that require looking up, too many arcane musical comedy references and too many quotes that are not as felicitous as he thinks. There is a glorious point in the working of a Double-Crostic when the puzzle falls together, you see what the quote is going to be about and you realize who the author is—and that moment is not so glorious when the quote is from *Phyllis Diller's Marriage Manual.*

I see that I am on the verge of blaming Thomas Middleton for my ineptitude at his puzzles, and I suppose that really isn't fair. I still like Double-Crostics. I sit with my dictionary and my atlas and eventually I solve them. In pencil. Erasing a lot. Still, I long for a giraffe's eye or two, and I remember the time Mrs. Wortman's definition said: "This really ought to be next to a church," and the answer was "laundry." That was nice. I miss it.

*May, 1977*

# The Sperling Breakfast

No one in Washington quite knows how Godfrey Sperling's breakfast group got to be quite the thing it has become. Godfrey Sperling himself, who started holding his breakfasts eleven years ago, claims to have no idea whatsoever. "I didn't set up a group," he said recently. "I just had a breakfast. And it wasn't even a breakfast. It was a lunch. Chuck Percy was coming to Washington, and he didn't know anyone, so I called up Bob Novak and Alan Otten and Peter Lisagor and three or four other reporters, and before I knew it I had twelve people. And they came. It made a lot of ripples, so I had another. And another. The second year I did it people started saying, You've got something this city needs. I said, I can't imagine it. But I kept having them. Each time I'd say, This will be the last one. After a while, people started saying it was an institution. I couldn't believe it. I couldn't believe it."

There have now been nearly eight hundred Sperling breakfasts, and thirty-seven members of the print press are invited to attend; over the years, they have met with almost every major American political figure. The Sperling Breakfast is indeed an institution. Some of its members think it's a good institution, useful and convenient, and that it would have to be invented if it did not exist. Others think it's a bad institution, dangerous and silly, and that it ought to be taken out like an old horse and shot. I'd like to tell you who said the line about the horse, but he asked not to be quoted. He doesn't want to hurt Godfrey Sperling's feelings. Also, he doesn't want Godfrey Sperling to throw him out of the breakfast group.

I recently spent a week in Washington attending five Sperling breakfasts. I had a wonderful time, except for the eggs. On Monday, Governor Jay Rockefeller of West Virginia was the guest. On Tuesday, Governor James "Big Jim" Thompson of Illinois. On Wednesday, Treasury Secretary Michael Blumenthal. On Thursday, White House counsel Robert Lipshutz. On Friday, Budget Director Bert Lance. I also interviewed many of the members of the breakfast group. I had a wonderful time doing that too. Everyone I spoke to was helpful. Many of them said it was only a breakfast. Sometimes it produces stories, sometimes it doesn't. That's not why it's valuable, they said. It's valuable because it provides an opportunity for the press to see how politicians perform. And why is it dangerous? I asked. It's dangerous, they said, because it's pack journalism and it can become a substitute for real reporting. This interested me, because it seemed to me they had it backward. The Sperling Breakfast is *valuable* because it's pack journalism and it does substitute for real reporting. And it's *dangerous* because it provides an opportunity for the press to see how politicians perform. How a politician performs does not prove anything about him except for his ability to hornswoggle journalists and pay his respects to their egos. But I'm getting carried away.

The Sperling Breakfast is supposed to be an informal way for politicians to meet with journalists, but it is actually a formal, ritualized, on-the-record press conference that happens to take place over breakfast. Columnists Joseph Kraft, Carl Rowan, David Broder and Robert Novak attend regularly. So do most of the bureau chiefs of the major news organizations—Mel Elfin of *Newsweek,* Hugh Sidey of *Time,* Jack Nelson of the *Los Angeles Times,* Jim Wieghart of the *New York Daily News,* Hedrick Smith of the *New York Times,* among others—and when they don't feel like coming they send their staff members. (Women are al-

lowed as substitutes, but there are only two female
regulars; representatives of the wire services and of television are banned.) Breakfast costs six dollars per member.

The group meets with a guest two or three morn-
ings a week at a long oval table in a banquet room of
the Sheraton Carlton Hotel. Godfrey Sperling, bureau
chief of the *Christian Science Monitor,* presides. At 8
a.m., he asks the first question. He also asks the second, third, fourth, fifth and sixth questions. Then he
calls on other members of the group. They ask questions. Sperling asks more questions. The guest answers
the questions. At three minutes to nine, Sperling calls
for "one last question." Then he calls for "the final
question." Then he calls for "the final final question."
Just after 9 a.m., the breakfast ends. If something has
happened at it, the reporters from the afternoon papers
run for the phones. The rest walk back to their offices,
comparing notes on what the story was, and complaining about the eggs.

Occasionally, major stories break at a Sperling
Breakfast. You've seen them: the second sentence
of the article says, "So-and-so made these remarks at a
breakfast with reporters." Bobby Kennedy agonized
over whether to run for President at a breakfast with
reporters; Spiro Agnew called Hubert Humphrey "soft
on Communism"; Earl Butz told a dirty joke about the
Pope: John Rhodes suggested that Nixon might be im-
peached. The breakfast is also an ideal launching pad
for trial balloons. In the last days of the Nixon administration, White House aide Patrick Buchanan used a
breakfast to test the strategy of conceding the House
of Representatives to pro-impeachment forces; by day's
end, the story was in the papers, along with negative responses from congressional leaders; Buchanan
realized the approach wouldn't work and junked
it.

Most of the time, however, nothing happens at a
Sperling Breakfast. This does not necessarily mean that

no stories are written. For example, here is what happened the day Big Jim Thompson appeared:

Governor Thompson was asked what he thought of President Carter's performance thus far. He said it was too soon to tell. He was asked about the future of the Republican party. He said that what the Republican party really needed was candidates who could win in 1978 and 1980. He was asked if he had the Presidential bug. "Sure," he said, "there's nothing new in that." Toward the end of breakfast, Warren Weaver of the *New York Times* turned to Andrew Glass of the Cox newspapers. "This guy is very impressive," he said.

Later in the day, I went to see Richard Dudman, bureau chief of the *St. Louis Post-Dispatch*. "I got a story today," he said. "I wrote that Governor Thompson met with the national press today and despite his disclaimers left no doubt that he's already running for President."

"What disclaimers?" I asked. "He admitted it. He has always admitted it."

"I know it," said Dudman. "I even called Springfield and they told me there's nothing new in it. But it's a story when he says it to us."

"You have to understand something," Jack Nelson of the *L.A. Times* said. "The first time Jimmy Carter was ever taken seriously in Washington was at a Sperling Breakfast."

I think I understand: You cannot be taken seriously in Washington *until* you have done the Sperling Breakfast. The Sperling Breakfast is a screening committee. But I'm getting carried away.

On Wednesday, Treasury Secretary Blumenthal came to the breakfast. He spoke of inflation, budget underruns and the New York financial mess. After breakfast, everyone agreed that he had performed well, and the reporters for afternoon papers ran for the phones. There would be front-page stories that afternoon and next morning. I walked over to the Treasury Building with Blumenthal's press aide, Treasury Assistant Secretary Joseph Laitin. "The session served a useful purpose for Blumenthal," Laitin said. "He wanted to talk to a cross section of the press to get a few things out. I didn't feel we should have a press conference because television always dominates it. You also get everybody in town, and if you don't produce eight-column headlines it's a letdown. We had a standing invitation from the Sperling people, so I called up and said we'd like to accept. Now about what Blumenthal said—there wasn't anything really new, yet it was important for these guys to hear it. All the financial reporters knew about the underruns and they've written about them, but none of them has dramatized it. They will now. Why haven't they before? Too unimaginative. Too lazy. Don't have the time. It's been out, but until now it hasn't been packaged. That's the word I want. Packaging."

Bob Strauss loves doing the Sperling Breakfast. He did nine of them as Democratic national chairman, and he invited the entire group to his home for dinner the day the five hundredth breakfast was held. Then along came the six hundredth Sperling Breakfast, and Gerald Ford invited everyone to the White House. That seemed like only yesterday, and suddenly the seven hundredth breakfast rolled around, and the eight hundredth is coming up. The members are getting grouchy; the anniversaries are getting closer and closer together; there are more and more breakfasts. No one minds getting up for somebody interesting, but the other day the group was actually asked to turn up for Senator Alan Cranston. Alan Cranston, for God's sake. The group has gotten too big; the group is too elite; the questions are too general; the questions are too specific. (The eggs are the only subject on which there is total agreement.) Even when Godfrey Sperling leaves town, the Sperling Breakfast goes on. Roscoe Drummond plays host, or Richard Strout. "It started out," says one of the original members, "and practically every guest was somebody you really wanted to see. But somewhere along the line it all became a Godfrey Sperling Production. He felt an obligation to serve up two guests a week, three guests a week, four guests a week. You turn out a lot of crap that way. He was producing guys you could walk up to the Hill and call off the floor at any time."

But I was talking about Bob Strauss, who loves doing the Sperling Breakfast. "I've grown very attached to it," he says. "I'll tell you why. I go in there with something to say and I say it. I bring in my medicine and I give it out. Some of them think it's red medicine, and some of them think it's blue medicine. But it tastes just fine."

Whenever there is a Sperling Breakfast, an announcement appears on the Sheraton Carlton bulletin board. BREAKFAST WITH GODFREY, 8 A.M., it reads. This is extremely embarrassing to Godfrey Sperling— not the announcement, you must understand, but the reference to his first name. Godfrey Sperling is not known as Godfrey. He is known as Budge. "I have two older sisters," he explained, "and they didn't care for the name Godfrey, and they called me Brother. Don't ask me how, but it became Budgie. I shortened it to Budge in college. The nice thing about the name Budge is it's informal. I never have been Godfrey. The name's been in my family and I use it as a by-line. But in my mind I'm always Budge Sperling."

Sperling, sixty-one, is a pleasant, fussy man who looks like Elmer Fudd and indeed occasionally gives the impression of being thoroughly befuddled. Here, for example, is a question he asked Budget Director Lance at Friday's breakfast: "Isn't what you really mean is that you're going to spend this defense money more slowly? Isn't that what you mean? More slowly?

Or is it less fastly? More slowly? You get me so dog-gone confused with all this. I'm just so doggone confused." Budge Sperling really enjoys his breakfasts. "It's a great help to me," he says. "The self-interest just oozes in every direction. But I've been engulfed by the thing. I can't tell if I'm running it or it's running me. This week I didn't want five, but I must admit I can't say no, I can't say no. This is a sideline that occupies me, interests me, irritates me. Sometimes it takes me over. If anyone had said to me, the thing you'll be remembered for is your breakfast group, I would have gone into another career. A breakfast group?"

I asked Sperling if he thought he was at all powerful. "Powerful?" he said. "I don't know. That's not Budge Sperling. It might be Godfrey Sperling, but not Budge. I have always felt that the Godfrey is too formal. It's not me."

In the course of a week, I heard a lot of things about the Sperling Breakfast. I was told that the whole purpose of the group was to promote peer approval and a feeling of joint accomplishment. I was told that the only reason anyone goes is for protection on those infrequent occasions when something interesting happens. I was even told that Godfrey Sperling had become so powerful he was dangerous. Well, I don't buy it. I think no one gives the Sperling Breakfast the credit it deserves. It provides a way for our politicians to get out of bed and come to show their dependence on the press; the press responds graciously by passing on exactly what the politicians come in to say. It provides a way for our politicians to pay tribute to the role of the press in the electoral process; the press reciprocates by certifying the politicians as heavyweights and contenders. It provides a way for the out-of-power party to survive those long stretches between elections; right now, while the rest of us lie around playing Scrabble, the Sperling Breakfast is doing its damnedest to find

Republican candidates for 1980. It even seems possible to say that the Sperling Breakfast is single-handedly saving the two-party system in America. But I'm getting carried away.

*June, 1977*

# Enough

I started to write this column about the new special sections in the *New York Times*. I had a nice lead for it, and I had a funny story to tell, and I had a few points to make about the Cuisinarting of America. I went over to the *Times* and had an amazing interview with a *Times* business executive who talked about something called psychographics. "One of the biggest psychographics," he said, "is self-improvement and self. Self is very strong." I also had a problem with the piece. About a year ago, I wrote something about the influence of city magazines on journalism, about the you-are-what-you-buy syndrome, and I didn't want to repeat myself. Oh, well. It really doesn't matter, because I decided not to write that column after all.

When I started writing a media column a couple of years ago, my primary interest was not to become a media critic—and I hope I have managed to succeed at not becoming one—but simply to find some subject to write about in order to get back into the front of *Esquire* magazine. I like being in the front of this magazine. It's nice up here. The subject of media was suggested over a lunch, and it seemed like a good idea. I could write about newspapers and magazines and television, and occasionally go out and do some reporting, and it might work. The reporting was the easy part. Journalists are wonderful sources. They are wonderful sources on the record, and they are even more wonderful sources off the record.

Those of us who work in this profession are very lucky, and we know it. I have known it ever since the day in 1963 when I walked into the *New York Post* city room to start work as a reporter: This is what I have always wanted, and here I am, and it's wonderful. I think this all the time. I am giddy about working in this profession. Every so often I hear someone complaining about how movies like *The Front Page* have tended to romanticize journalism, and I don't understand what they're talking about. I grew up under the influence of a remake of *The Front Page—His Girl Friday,* in which Rosalind Russell played the Hildy Johnson part. I grew up wanting to be Hildy Johnson, and as it turns out, Hildy Johnson is someone worth wanting to grow up to be.

In recent years, however, there have been some changes. One of them has to do with celebrity. Journalists are now celebrities. Part of this has been caused by the ability and willingness of journalists to promote themselves. Part of this has been caused by television: the television reporter is often more famous than anyone he interviews. And part of this has been caused by the fact that the celebrity pool has expanded in order to provide names to fill the increasing number of column inches currently devoted to gossip; this is my own pet theory, and I use it to explain all sorts of things, one of whom is Halston.

The point, though, is that the extent to which a column like this contributes to this makes me extremely uncomfortable; what's more, this development of celebrity has been reinforced by a parallel change in journalism, a swing from highly impersonal "objective" reporting to highly personal "subjective" reporting. Last week, while preparing for the column on the *New York Times* I decided not to write, I reread the last few months of the "Weekend," "Living" and "Home" sections of the *Times,* and I began to overdose on the first person singular pronoun. I am tired of the first person singular pronoun. I am tired of reading about how this journalist serves her guests dinner on the bed and about how that journalist has a Shetland pony with a nervous tic. I am also tired of my own first person singular pronoun. "Self is very strong," said the *Times* business executive. Yes indeed. I figure if

I stop writing a column for a while, it will reduce the number of first person singular pronouns in circulation by only a hair; still, it seems like the noblest thing I can think of to do this week.

David Eisenhower once said something that made me realize that he could not possibly be as silly as he seems. "Journalists," he said, "aren't nearly as interesting as they think they are." Actually, he's not quite right. Journalists *are* interesting. They just aren't as interesting as the things they cover. It is possible to lose sight of this.

I would like not to.

*July, 1977*

## ABOUT THE AUTHOR

NORA EPHRON is a contributing editor of *Esquire*. Her work has appeared in *New York* magazine, *Rolling Stone, Ms., The New York Times Book Review,* and *The New Yorker*. She is also the author of *Wallflower at the Orgy* and *Crazy Salad*. She lives in New York and Washington with her husband, Carl Bernstein.

# We Deliver!

## And So Do These Bestsellers.

| | | | |
|---|---|---|---|
| ☐ | 11256 | **HAYWIRE** by Brooke Hayward | $2.50 |
| ☐ | 12261 | **DR. SHEEHAN ON RUNNING** by George A. Sheehan, M.D. | $2.25 |
| ☐ | 12528 | **GODS FROM OUTER SPACE** by Erich Von Daniken | $2.25 |
| ☐ | 12868 | **LINDA GOODMAN'S SUN SIGNS** | $2.75 |
| ☐ | 11162 | **THE DAVID KOPAY STORY** by David Kopay & Perry Young | $1.95 |
| ☐ | 12427 | **THE MOTHER EARTH NEWS ALMANAC** by John Shuttleworth | $2.50 |
| ☐ | 12220 | **LIFE AFTER LIFE** by Ramond Moody, M.D. | $2.25 |
| ☐ | 11150 | **THE BOOK OF LISTS** by D. Wallechinsky, I. & A. Wallace | $2.50 |
| ☐ | 11255 | **GUINNESS BOOK OF WORLD RECORDS** 16th Ed. by the McWhirters | $2.25 |
| ☐ | 12331 | **WHAT DO YOU SAY AFTER YOU SAY HELLO?** by Dr. Eric Berne | $2.50 |
| ☐ | 11979 | **BURY MY HEART AT WOUNDED KNEE** by Dee Brown | $2.75 |
| ☐ | 12196 | **PASSAGES** by Gail Sheehy | $2.75 |
| ☐ | 11656 | **KICKING THE FEAR HABIT** by Manuel J. Smith | $2.25 |
| ☐ | 12218 | **THE GREATEST MIRACLE IN THE WORLD** by Og Mandino | $1.95 |
| ☐ | 12250 | **ALL CREATURES GREAT AND SMALL** by James Herriot | $2.50 |
| ☐ | 11001 | **DR. ATKINS' DIET REVOLUTION** by Dr. Robert Atkins | $2.25 |
| ☐ | 12533 | **THE PETER PRINCIPLE** by Peter & Hull | $2.25 |
| ☐ | 11291 | **THE LATE GREAT PLANET EARTH** by Hal Lindsey | $1.95 |
| ☐ | 11400 | **WHEN I SAY NO, I FEEL GUILTY** by Manuel Smith | $2.25 |

**Buy them at your local bookstore or use this handy coupon for ordering:**

Bantam Books, Inc., Dept. NFB, 414 East Golf Road, Des Plaines, Ill. 60016

Please send me the books I have checked above. I am enclosing $_____ (please add 75¢ to cover postage and handling). Send check or money order —no cash or C.O.D.'s please.

Mr/Mrs/Miss_____

Address_____

City_____State/Zip_____

NFB—2/79

Please allow four weeks for delivery. This offer expires 8/79.

# LEARNING TO WRITE AND ENJOYING IT

Books that can help you improve your ability to communicate. The interested beginning writer will find valuable direction and hints about how to write more efficiently and creatively.

☐ 10108   **HOW TO ACHIEVE COMPETENCE IN ENGLISH**   $1.50

☐ 11857   **LIFE INTO LANGUAGE**   $1.95

☐ 10186   **PICTURES FOR WRITING**   $1.50

☐ 10201   **SHORT STORY WRITING**   $1.25

☐ 10437   **THE WRITER'S EYE**   $1.50

☐ 12379   **WRITING IN GENERAL AND THE SHORT STORY IN PARTICULAR**   $2.50

☐ 11529   **WRITING AND RESEARCHING TERM PAPERS**   $1.95

**Buy them at your local bookstore or use this handy coupon for ordering:**

---

**Bantam Books, Inc., Dept. WR, 414 East Golf Road, Des Plaines, Ill. 60016**

Please send me the books I have checked above. I am enclosing $_____
(please add 75¢ to cover postage and handling). Send check or money order—no cash or C.O.D.'s please.

Mr/Mrs/Miss _____

Address _____

City _____ State/Zip _____

WR—1/79

Please allow four weeks for delivery. This offer expires 7/79.